DEHYDRATOR COOKBOOK FOR PREPPERS

A Practical Guide to Dehydrating Fruits, Vegetables, Meat, Fish, Bread and Other Food Items for Stockpiling and Emergency Situations

Monroe Canning

© Copyright 2023

All rights reserved.

The contents of this book may not be reproduced, duplicated, or transmitted without a written permission directly from the author or the publisher. Under no circumstances will any fault or legal liability will be attributed to the publisher, or the author, for any damages, compensation or monetary loss due directly or indirectly to the information contained in this book.

Legal Notice:

This book is copyrighted. This book is for personal use only. You may not modify, distribute, sell, use, quote or paraphrase any part of the content, or the content itself within this book, without the written consent of the author or the publisher.

Table of Contents

BONUSES

DOWNLOAD INSTANTLY AND START EXPLORING A WORLD OF FLAVOR WITH YOUR BONUS RECIPE COLLECTIONS – EACH CRAFTED TO COMPLEMENT YOUR NEW DEHYDRATING SKILLS PERFECTLY. DON'T MISS OUT ON THESE DELECTABLE ADDITIONS TO YOUR CULINARY LIBRARY!

SCAN HERE TO DOWNLOAD THEM

Introduction

What is Dehydration?

Not only have humans hunted and collected food since the beginning of time; we have also preserved it. There is nothing new in extending the shelf life of the food we grow or buy. By drying the food we make sure that there is always something available in the closet that is good and nutritious to eat. If you've never thought about drying food before, once you find out how much fun it is, you may not be able to re-milk or freeze the food again.

There is a good chance that one of your ancestors will dry things like fruits and vegetables. In fact, it is the oldest method of storing food.

Early civilizations used the sun and wind to dry berries, roots and even herbs. Native American tribes and early American settlers dried food to survive both the drought and the harsh winters.

Dehydration may seem complicated, but the process is simple.

Food has high water content. When food is dried, most of this water is removed, which prevents the growth of organisms such as yeasts, enzymes and bacteria, which all lead to deterioration. Fruits and vegetables are made up of about 80-95 percent water and meats are made up of 50-75 percent water. Dehydration reduces the water content to about 10 percent, leaving most of the complete nutritional value of food intact. Dehydration also acts as a natural food preservative.

What Foods Can Be Dehydrated

Almost any food that has moisture in it can be dried. You can dehydrate your vegetables, herbs, fruits, meats and fish. The dehydrated food can later be rehydrated to restore the water content, or some can be eaten dry.

When dehydrated, most fruits will turn leathery and the vegetables might become brittle or hard to touch.

We can retain most of the flavor in the herbs like parsley, mint, oregano, and basil by preserving them. You have the choice of using them fresh in the summer when they are abundant or using them dry in winter.

You can get fresh fish, which contains less fat, to dehydrate and make fish jerky by salt curing them.

Meat can be dehydrated to make jerky, which can either be rehydrated later when you cook it, of if you are travelling, you can eat it dry too.

Which Foods Cannot Be Dehydrated

The following foods do not dehydrate well:

- Avocados
- Olives
- Lean Meats
- The potential for getting sick from eating there is not worth it.
- Milk, butter, and cheese should be avoided.
- Nuts Peanut Butter
- Carbonated Drinks

When dehydrating meat, you should remove all visible fat. Only lean meat, poultry, or fish should be used for dehydrating. Ground meat should be no more than 10 percent fat. Fish like salmon and mackerel have **too high** a fat content to make them good candidates for dehydrating; they can be dried for short-term storage, but they should not be used for long-term storage due to the increased risk of spoilage.

Foods high in sugar or alcohol won't dry properly. Foods like alcohol-soaked fruit, honey, or candy tend to absorb moisture from the air and resist dehydration.

Benefits of Dehydration

Dehydration not only preserves food for a longer duration, but it is also responsible for making the food nutrients and delicious. The texture of the dried food is also enjoyable. It makes an excellent snack and an on-the-go meal to provide energy instantly. Here are some other benefits of drying food that you might find interesting:

Save Money

To start, you can save money. If you grow your own fruits and veggies, you can experience the "I can't look at another zucchini" blues at the end of the summer. You might feel pressured to let the green squash die on the vine or put them into the compost when you've had your fill of ratatouille and zucchini bread and your friends and neighbors see you heading their way with them in hand. And six months from now, the same thing will cost you $4 per pound.

By dehydrating those zucchinis, you are effectively depositing those cost-free or inexpensive calories, nutrients, and deliciousness into a savings account that you may use as you like for the remainder of the year.

You don't even need a garden to save money utilizing dehydration. From farm stands, farmers' markets, or shops that carry local produce, you can purchase food in bulk while it is freshest and most affordable and preserve it for the off-season. It's a gourmet take on the old stock market adage "buy low, sell high." With the exception that this time, you're eating rather than selling.

Minimize Food Waste

Another advantage of dehydrating food is that it reduces food waste. You may "upcycle" calories instead of letting them go bad and ending up in the compost or, worse, the garbage, whether you're using store-bought or home-grown food. If you have an abundance of vegetables and don't know what to do with them, consider dehydrating them. The shelf life of fruits and vegetables is significantly increased as a result, and you can utilize them whenever it is most convenient for you. It is preferable to dehydrate produce whilst it is still in its fresh state as opposed to waiting till it is partially spoiled as this will result in a greater amount of cleanup.

Takes Less Room

Dehydrating food can also save space. Depending on the water content of the item, dehydrating fruits and vegetables removes the water, which might reduce their size by 50%. If you dry your apples, you can store them in a tiny fraction of the space that they would require when they are fresh, even if you don't have a root cellar or a big refrigerator. Additionally, you won't need to occupy valuable counter or refrigerator space because dehydrated apples are less picky about where they should be stored.

Make Non-perishable Food

And finally, dried foods are virtually unbreakable. They preserve for a long time and don't require electricity or refrigeration to stay safe and delicious, making them excellent for disaster preparedness. Even if you aren't preparing for a year's worth of dining in the absence of farms, supermarkets, or gardens, dehydrated meals are fantastic for camping or bringing on lengthy vacations or travel where you don't have access to cooking equipment. Some campers dehydrate entire meals, rehydrate them when they have access to water and heat, and then enjoy them because dried food is portable and won't deteriorate.

Methods of Dehydration

There are several ways to dehydrate or dry food. Which one you select will depend on where you live, the climate, equipment, and the fresh produce you wish to dry.

Sun Drying

While this is the oldest method, it's not an option for many of us. You need to live in an area that is hot and dry and has long hrs of sunny daylight. Sun drying is not possible if you are located somewhere with patchy or limited sun or relative humidity greater than 20%.

This method is commonly used for drying fruit. Produce drying in the sun should be placed, preferably in a single layer, on mesh racks or fabric that allows the free circulation of air. Produce must be kept clean, protected from birds and flies, and turned occasionally.

I do not suggest using old window screens (or new screens for that matter) as they contain heavy metals or fiberglass that could leach onto your food. Only use food-safe materials.

Oven drying

This is the most energy greedy method and adds to your household costs. Another disadvantage is that foods dried this way can be less flavorful and more brittle. It's also relatively easy to move from dried food to burnt food. If you don't have an oven with a fan, it's slower than a dehydrator. You also need an oven with a "warm" setting or one that can go as low as 140 °Fahrenheit. Any warmer, and you are cooking, not drying!

Place produce in a single layer on oven trays or wire cooling racks (covered with cloth or netting) that are narrower than the width of your oven. There must be 2 ½ - 3 inches between trays. This allows air to circulate freely around the trays. Keep the oven door open 4 – 5 inches to improve airflow. Place a fan in front of the oven, especially if you don't have a fan-assisted oven, and ensure the kitchen is well ventilated.

Solar drying

There are very few fruits and vegetables that you can't dry this way, although those containing higher moisture contents, such as tomatoes, take longer. They are also great for herbs and mushrooms. There are two types: direct solar dryers and indirect solar food dryers.

Direct versions are simple and consist of one container protected on three sides by screens or sheeting. The fourth side is used to insert and remove the trays. The sun's UV rays are used to dry the food, boosted by the warmth generated inside the drying chamber. The disadvantages are loss of nutritional value and the danger of mold, both due to the slowness of the technique.

Indirect types have two chambers and dry food faster. They are called "indirect" because food is not directly exposed to sunshine. It is dried by the movement of hot air through the drying chamber that holds the trays of food. Below the drying chamber is a box lined with solar absorbers which collect solar energy and heat up the air.

This hot air then rises up through the drying chamber. Because the hot air moves constantly, the moisture released by the food is carried away and out. As the air is drawn in, the temperature can rise by as much as 20 °higher than the outside temperature. This hot air rises into the drying chamber and the moisture released leaves through the vents in the glazed glass or plastic roof.

You can buy a solar drying kit, a completed one, or build your own from scratch. The prices range from around $140 for a basic model up to approximately $800 for a full bells-and-whistles version. If you build one with all new materials you are looking at around $300. Regardless of the type you buy or build, here are a few hacks that will help to prevent waste and save you some time:

- Monitor temperatures. The ideal range is 120 – 140 °Fahrenheit.
- Swap the upper and lower trays if one is drying faster than the other.
- Bring the trays indoors if they are still not dry by evening. You don't want cool, moist night air to rehydrate the food.

Electric dehydrators

These produce the best quality dried food and are much faster and cheaper to run than traditional ovens. An electric dehydrator contains a heat source, trays to place produce on, and a ventilation system. Like with many modern kitchen appliances, there is a range available, and you can choose the one that best suits your needs. They can be expensive, but the investment is worth it because it saves you time and running costs and the final product is high quality.

As with the other methods, lay out food in single layers. Turn larger pieces halfway through the drying cycle, and move those on the edges to the center. Stir the small pieces to prevent sticking and clumping. All these measures allow the food to dry uniformly. The manufacturers of these machines provide guidelines for temperature and times for various food types.

Air-drying

This is also an age-old method. While you could hang bunches or bags of produce such as herbs and mushrooms outside if it's warm and dry, most of us do our air drying indoors. The best places are well ventilated and where the air is dry and could be an attic, a porch, or any space where air moves freely.

You can string herbs up in bunches or place them in paper bags to keep the food free of dust and other debris. You should bag your mushrooms.

Microwave drying

This is a quick method but only works (a) for small quantities and (b) for a limited number of types of produce. I'm not a fan of this method as the food often has a slightly strange taste. Some people use the microwave to dry herbs but be sure to keep an eye on it, or they could catch fire! I've never known this to happen to anyone personally, but it is something to keep in mind.

Which method or equipment you opt for will probably reflect your lifestyle, location, and budget.

How To Use Your Dehydrator

Pretreatments

As wonderful as it would be to just cut up some fruit and throw it in the dehydrator, that's not how this works. Some products require you to inactivate their enzymes before you start the drying process. So, what does inactivating enzymes entail exactly? It's just a fancy way of saying we don't want our produce to go brown. There are many different types of pretreatments, so make sure to research what will work best for your specific food before you start. The results of pretreatment can vary so feel free to test out what flavors and qualities you like best.

One pretreatment that is commonly used is called the natural pretreatment. This is when you add fruit juices to reduce browning in produce. Oftentimes, this is done with lime, lemon, orange, or pineapple juice. The ascorbic acid in these juices breaks down the enzymes that cause discoloration. Some places sell ascorbic acid mixture that does the job just as well in case you have an allergy to the natural juices. To make sure the fruit is entirely protected, soak it in your chosen ascorbic acid juice for at least 5 mins before putting it in the dehydrator. You can also use a mixture of honey and juice, or just honey on its own.

Another type of pretreatment is syrup blanching. To do this, start by mixing a cup of sugar with a cup of white corn syrup and 2 cups of water. This will become your sugar syrup. Next, boil the sugar syrup and add your slices of fresh fruit. Let this simmer for 10 mins on low heat. Remove the mixture from the heat source but allow the fruit to stand in the syrup for another 30-45 mins. Then drain and rinse the fruit lightly with cold water. Syrup blanching makes the fruit sweet due to the absorption of some sugar. This also contributes to its sticky texture. While this pretreatment results in a delicious taste, it's not exactly the healthiest.

The next pretreatment is sulfating. This is the process of soaking fruit in a solution of sodium bisulfite. Dissolve 1 tablespoon of sodium bisulfite in 1 gallon of water and soak the fruit for 5-10 mins. Rinse the fruit off before placing it in the dehydrator. As you can probably tell from the name sodium bisulfite, this method is high in sodium, and it isn't recommended for those on a low sodium diet. It's also potentially harmful to people with asthma or other respiratory issues. Sodium bisulfite is used in wine-making and can be obtained from stores that supply those materials.

If you're more preoccupied with flavor than browning, you can also use garnishes as a pretreatment. Just add some spices, gelatin, or coconut to the fresh fruit you have prepared to give it an extra kick. Some popular options are granola, chopped nuts, poppy seeds, sesame seeds, or sunflower seeds. Garnishes work best if paired with the natural pretreatment. The honey or ascorbic acid fruit juice helps the garnish adhere better to the fruit. If you choose to do this, you don't have to soak the fruit for a full 5 mins. You can just dip it in before applying the garnish.

Dehydration

Once all your produce has gone through the proper pretreatments, it's time to start dehydrating. The entire point of drying out your food is to make sure there's nothing for the microorganisms to feast upon. Since the dehydrator isn't a magical machine, you'll need to make sure that this process can be successfully done. Make sure the product isn't going into the dehydrator excessively wet, or into puddles of its own oil. This will make the drying process take longer than necessary. Certain kinds of meat might have this problem, so make sure to blot it down with a dry paper towel.

Keep in mind as you are slicing your produce that the smaller the pieces are, the shorter the drying time will be. However, just because your pieces are small, doesn't mean you can crowd the trays. It's important to evenly space whatever you are drying. Air needs to circulate between the food pieces, and not just on the top and bottom. If you are drying fruit leather, don't pour the puree unevenly, or it will come out with an undesirable texture. If your trays are stackable, place the items you want to dry faster at the bottom. You can dry different products at once but just make sure you are using the safest temperature.

Once your trays are filled, close the lid/door. Set the temperature to the recommended setting. Depending on your model, your dehydrator might have a digital display or a dial. Either way, you should be able to manually change it. For most meat, this will be 160 degrees Fahrenheit. If you are cooking poultry, it's going to be 165 degrees Fahrenheit. Fruit and vegetables dry at much lower temperatures. Fruit dries at 135 degrees while vegetables dry at 130 degrees Fahrenheit.

Sit tight because the next step is going to take a long time. Drying food can last anywhere between a few hrs and a few days. Some dehydrators have timers on them that can help remind you when the food is ready. Not all dehydrators have this convenience though. You can use an old-fashioned kitchen timer for that vintage feel, or you could just set an alarm on your phone. Dehydrators with stackable trays sometimes need the bottom switched out for better drying circulation, so don't forget to do that as well. You'll also want to check in on your food periodically to make sure everything is going according to plan.

As your time gets closer to the end, check on your food more often. You don't want to over-dry the product and ruin the flavor and texture. You'll know your fruit is done once it becomes nice and leathery. If it's still a little sticky, let it go a little while longer. Vegetables will snap and break cleanly. Jerky should crack but not break, and just like fruit, it should be leathery. Give the dehydrator a little time to cool before you take your goodies out. It's normal to be excited but you don't want to burn yourself. Most importantly wear an oven mitt.

How to Rehydrate Foods

If you do not use dehydrated food as a seasoning (herbs, for example) or snacks (like beef jerky or fruit leathers), you will use them in cooking. But how do you rehydrate food so that you get the best results? There are several methods:

- **Add to a dish:** Add dehydrated vegetables and herbs to soups, stews, curries, a vegetable bake, or pasta sauce. The vegetables will rehydrate during the cooking process.

- **Boil in a bag:** Place foods or food mixes such as vegetables and rice into mylar bags that are food grade and heat rated for 212 ⁰ Fahrenheit and above. Add boiling water to the bag, seal it, and leave it to rehydrate. Stir it after about 10 mins to ensure all the ingredients are in contact with the water. This method takes 15 – 20 mins. This is particularly useful when you are camping or hiking. Please note that not all mylar bags are created equal! Some bags should not be used with boiling water. Check the company website or specifically buy bags that are food grade and approved to use with boiling water.

- **Soak and simmer:** Place the food and water into a pot and leave it to soak for thirty mins or so. Turn on the flame and simmer until all the food is rehydrated. This is useful for one-pot meals such as vegetable rice.

Of course, you can eat some dehydrated foods, such as fruit, exactly as they are; no rehydration is required!

FAQ

What is the shelf life of dehydrated food?

Although properly prepared and kept dried food has indeed been known to survive five to 10 years, it's preferable to utilize yours between four months to 12 months.

Are nutrients lost (or preserved) when food is dehydrated?

Food may lose some nutrients when it is dried, but not as much as when it is preserved in another way. Vitamins break down because of light & heat. In other words, canning results in a greater loss of nutrients than low-humidity & heat dehydration. By blanching select veggies, you may lessen the quantity of vitamins A, C & thiamine that are lost from your diet.

Does food dehydration eradicate bacteria?

You may get rid of the bacteria that make food rot by drying the veggies and fruits until their moisture content is between 5-20 percent. The USDA suggests first cooking raw meat to 160 F and then drying at a specific temp of 145 F if you're concerned about germs on meat.

Does the food that has been dried have more sugar?

As dehydrating concentrates sugar while eliminating water vapor, dried fruit feels sweeter. Dried fruit has more sugar per g than fresh fruit, although total sugar content is not increased by drying fruit.

Does food dehydration destroy enzymes?

Yes, in certain instances. Yes, enzymes do die when food is dried at extreme temps. Denser foods can endure greater temps without losing enzymes, but when temps above 140-158 F, most enzymes ultimately lose their activity.

Can you use an Instant Pot to dehydrate food?

Sadly, no. Even though an Instant Pot is a fantastic multi-tool that can slow cook, cook under pressure, and make yogurt, it is too damp to dry anything. Despite the lid being open.

Can cooked food be dehydrated?

You can, indeed. Even meals can be dried, but certain cooked foods dry better than some others.

How should I keep dry goods stored?

Pack the food into silicone bags or freezer-safe containers with tight-fitting covers, or keep it in dry, clean jars (simple mason jars or canning jars can work well).

CHAPTER 1: Recipes for Vegetables

DEHYDRATED ASPARAGUS

PREPARATION TIME	COOKING TIME	SERVING
10 mins	6 hrs	2

INGREDIENTS	DIRECTIONS
• 4 cups asparagus, clipped & cut	1. Arrange the asparagus in the food dehydrator. 2. Process at 125 degrees F for 6 hrs. 3. Storage suggestions: store in a sealable plastic bag. **Tip:** you can also season the asparagus with salt or garlic powder.

PER SERVING			
Calories: 434kcal	**Fat:** 39.4g	**Carbs:** 20.9g	**Protein:** 5.8g

MAPLE CARROT STRAWS

PREPARATION TIME	COOKING TIME	SERVING
15 mins	6 hrs	4

INGREDIENTS	DIRECTIONS
• one lb. Carrots, cut into long strips • one tbsp. maple syrup • one tablespoon olive oil • Salt to taste	1. Combine all the ingredients in a container. 2. Arrange the strips in the food dehydrator. 3. Process at 135 degrees F for 6 hrs. 4. Storage suggestions: store in a food container. **Tip:** use a peeler to slice the carrots.

PER SERVING			
Calories: 214kcal	**Fat:** 3g	**Carbs:** 41g	**Protein:** 4.3g

ZUCCHINI SNACKS

PREPARATION TIME	COOKING TIME	SERVING
45 mins	12 hrs	4

INGREDIENTS	DIRECTIONS
• 8 zucchinis, sliced into rounds and seeds removed • 1 cup grape juice concentrate • 1 cup water	1. Place all the ingredients to a pot over medium heat. 2. Bring to a boil. 3. Reduce heat and simmer for 30 mins. 4. Drain the zucchini and let cool. 5. Add the zucchinis to the food dehydrator. 6. Process at 135 degrees F for 12 hrs. 7. Storage suggestions: store in the refrigerator for up to 1 week. **Tip:** do not overcook the zucchinis.

PER SERVING			
Calories: 9kcal	**Fat:** 0g	**Carbs:** 2.1g	**Protein:** 0.2g

CUCUMBER CHIPS

PREPARATION TIME	COOKING TIME	SERVING
15 mins	6 hrs	4

INGREDIENTS	DIRECTIONS
• 3 cucumber, cut into rounds • one tbsp. avocado oil • 2 teaspoons apple cider vinegar • Salt to taste	1. Toss the cucumber slices in avocado oil and vinegar. 2. Season with the salt. 3. Add the cucumber slices to the food dehydrator. 4. Dehydrate at 135 degrees F for 6 hrs. 5. Storage suggestions: store in an airtight container. **Tip:** you can use a mandoline slicer to slice the cucumbers thinly. Dry the cucumber slices with a paper towel before processing.

PER SERVING			
Calories: 9kcal	**Fat:** 0g	**Carbs:** 2.1g	**Protein:** 0.2g

DEHYDRATED OKRA

PREPARATION TIME	COOKING TIME	SERVING
15 mins	12 hrs	4

INGREDIENTS	DIRECTIONS
• 12 okra, sliced	1. Add the okra to the food dehydrator. 2. Dry at 130 degrees F for 12 hrs. 3. Storage suggestions: store in an airtight container. **Tip**: drizzle with powdered herb or spice for added flavor.

PER SERVING			
Calories: 70kcal	**Fat:** 4g	**Carbs:** 30g	**Protein:** 2g

SWEET KALE CHIPS

PREPARATION TIME	COOKING TIME	SERVING
15 mins	6 hrs	4

INGREDIENTS	DIRECTIONS
• 1 bunch curly kale, washed, tough stems eliminated and leaves roughly torn • ½ cup pine nuts • 1/8-1/4 cup white sugar • ½ tbsp. Cinnamon • 1/3 cup water • 1/8 cup apple cider vinegar	1. Put pine nuts, sugar and cinnamon inside a food processor. 2. Blend water and vinegar and add slowly to food processor. 3. Pour mixture over kale and mix until coated. 4. Place on dehydrating trays for 2-4 hrs at 140 degrees F.

PER SERVING			
Calories: 108kcal	**Fat:** 7.9g	**Carbs:** 9.4g	**Protein:** 1.9g

DRIED SWEET POTATO

PREPARATION TIME	COOKING TIME	SERVING
10 mins	12 hrs	4

INGREDIENTS	DIRECTIONS
• 2 sweet potatoes • 1 teaspoon onion powder	1. Season the sweet potato slices with onion powder. 2. Arrange in a single layer in the food dehydrator. 3. Set at 115 degrees F. 4. Process for 12 hrs. 5. Storage suggestions: store in a sealable plastic bag. **Tip**: use a mandolin slicer to prepare the sweet potatoes.

PER SERVING			
Calories: 108kcal	**Fat:** 7.9g	**Carbs:** 9.4g	**Protein:** 1.9g

CARROT CAKE

PREPARATION TIME	COOKING TIME	SERVING
30 mins	9 hrs	6

INGREDIENTS	DIRECTIONS
• 3 cups carrots, grated • 1 teaspoon cinnamon • 1/2 teaspoon nutmeg • 1/4 teaspoon ground cloves • 1 cup pecans, crushed • 1/2 cup shredded coconut • 1/4 cup water • 1/2 teaspoon salt	1. In a food processor, mix the pecans and coconut and pulse. 2. In a large container, combine the carrots, pecans, coconut, cinnamon, nutmeg, cloves, water, and salt. 3. Place ParaFlexx Screens on the racks of your Food Dehydrator. 4. Form the dough into individual cakes about 4 inches across. Place the cakes onto the screens and set your Food dehydrator to 165 F. Dehydrate for one hour, then lower the temperature to 125F and dehydrate for another 8 hrs.

PER SERVING			
Calories: 211kcal	**Fat:** 19g	**Carbs:** 10.2g	**Protein:** 3.2g

DRIED CAULIFLOWER POPCORN

PREPARATION TIME	COOKING TIME	SERVING
15 mins	8 hrs	1

INGREDIENTS	DIRECTIONS
<ul><li>two cups cauliflower florets</li><li>4 tablespoons hot sauce</li><li>3 tablespoons coconut oil</li><li>one tsp. smoked cayenne</li><li>half tsp. ground cumin</li><li>one tbsp. paprika</li></ul>	1. Toss the cauliflower florets in hot sauce and coconut oil. 2. Drizzle with the smoked cayenne, cumin and paprika. 3. Add the seasoned cauliflower to the food dehydrator. 4. Dry at 130 deg. F for 8 hrs. 5. Store in an airtight plastic bag. **Tip:** add more cayenne pepper for spicier cauliflower popcorn.

PER SERVING			
Calories: 9kcal	**Fat:** 0g	**Carbs:** 2.1g	**Protein:** 0.2g

SPINACH BALLS

PREPARATION TIME	COOKING TIME	SERVING
15 mins	6 hrs	4

INGREDIENTS	DIRECTIONS
<ul><li>three cups cashews</li><li>three cups blanched spinach</li><li>4 tbsp. Olive oil</li><li>quarter cup dehydrated onion flakes</li><li>three cloves garlic</li><li>¼ tsp. Nutmeg</li><li>Pinch of cayenne pepper</li></ul>	1. Process the cashews until they are finely ground. Add all the remaining ingredients and pulse several times until well combined and paste-like in consistency. 2. Pour mixture into a container and form into small, bite-size balls. 3. Place spinach balls on dehydrator sheets and dehydrate at 120 degrees F for 5 hrs.

PER SERVING			
Calories: 137kcal	**Fat:** 10.5g	**Carbs:** 9.2g	**Protein:** 3.7g

DEHYDRATED TOMATOES

PREPARATION TIME	COOKING TIME	SERVING
20 mins	8 hrs	2

INGREDIENTS	DIRECTIONS
<ul><li>Two tomatoes, cut into quarters</li><li>Salt as required</li></ul>	1. Add the tomatoes to the food dehydrator. 2. Drizzle with salt. 3. Set to 135 degrees F. 4. Process for 8 hrs. 5. Storage suggestions: store in a sealable plastic bag. Squeeze out the air. Store for around 2 months in a cool dry place. 6. Freeze then store for up to 6 months. **Tip**: don't forget to scrape the seeds before drying.

PER SERVING			
Calories: 250kcal	Fat: 7.6g	Carbs: 41g	Protein: 4.5g

DEHYDRATED BEETS

PREPARATION TIME	COOKING TIME	SERVING
20 mins	12 hrs	4

INGREDIENTS	DIRECTIONS
<ul><li>three beets, cut finely</li><li>¼ cup water</li><li>¼ cup vinegar</li><li>1 tablespoon olive oil</li><li>Salt to taste</li></ul>	1. Combine all the ingredients in a container. 2. Marinate for 10 mins. 3. Arrange the beet slices in the food dehydrator. 4. Dehydrate at 135 degrees F for 12 hrs. 5. Storage suggestions: store in a sealable plastic bag. **Tip**: use a mandoliner slicer to slice the beets thinly.

PER SERVING			
Calories: 70kcal	Fat: 4g	Carbs: 30g	Protein: 2g

SPICED CUCUMBERS

PREPARATION TIME	COOKING TIME	SERVING
20 mins	4 hrs	2

INGREDIENTS	DIRECTIONS
• two cucumbers, cut into rounds • two teaspoons olive oil • 2 teaspoons vinegar • 1 tablespoon paprika • two tsps. onion powder • two tsps. garlic powder • two tsps. sugar • Pinch chili powder	1. Toss the cucumbers in oil and vinegar. 2. Drizzle with the sugar and spices. 3. Put the cucumber slices in the food dehydrator. 4. Process at 135 degrees F for 6 hrs. 5. Storage suggestions: store in an airtight container. **Tip**: dehydrate longer if you want your cucumber crispier.

PER SERVING			
Calories: 250kcal	**Fat:** 7.6g	**Carbs:** 41.8g	**Protein:** 4.5g

DEHYDRATED CORN

PREPARATION TIME	COOKING TIME	SERVING
10 mins	12 hrs	4

INGREDIENTS	DIRECTIONS
• 8 cups corn kernels	1. Spread the corn kernels in the food dehydrator. 2. Process at 125 degrees F for 12 hrs. 3. Storage suggestions: store in a glass jar with lid. **Tip**: you can also drizzle the corn kernels in olive oil before dehydrating.

PER SERVING			
Calories: 214kcal	**Fat:** 3g	**Carbs:** 41.4g	**Protein:** 4.3g

SWEET AND SAVORY BEET ROUNDS

PREPARATION TIME	COOKING TIME	SERVING
15 mins	6 hrs	4

INGREDIENTS	DIRECTIONS
<ul><li>four large beets, washed</li><li>two tbsp. Olive oil</li><li>one teaspoon Fresh rosemary, finely sliced</li><li>half teaspoon Sea salt</li><li>quarter teaspoon Pepper</li></ul>	1. Cut tops of beets. Slice beets about 1/8-1/4 inch wide. Use a mandolin if possible. 2. Toss beets, olive oil, rosemary, salt and pepper in a container until evenly coated. 3. Set the dehydrator to 145 degrees F. Place trays in dehydrator for 10-12 hrs.

PER SERVING			
Calories: 21kcal	Fat: 0.5g	Carbs: 4.6g	Protein: 0.6g

MOROCCAN CARROT CRUNCH

PREPARATION TIME	COOKING TIME	SERVING
15 mins	6 hrs	4

INGREDIENTS	DIRECTIONS
<ul><li>1 pound of carrots, peeled</li><li>four tbsps. Olive oil</li><li>one tablespoon Honey</li><li>one-eighth teaspoon Cayenne pepper</li><li>2 tsp. Cumin</li><li>one teaspoon Dried parsley flakes</li><li>½ tsp. Salt</li></ul>	1. Wash, dry and thinly slice carrots. 2. Mix together oil, honey, and seasonings. 3. Place carrots onto dehydrator trays. Using a pastry brush, dab the mixture onto the carrot rounds. 4. Dehydrate for 6 hrs at 125 degrees F or until crisp.

PER SERVING			
Calories: 26kcal	Fat: 0.3g	Carbs: 6g	Protein: 0.5g

RANCH BRUSSELS SPROUT SKINS

PREPARATION TIME	COOKING TIME	SERVING
15 mins	6 hrs	4

INGREDIENTS	DIRECTIONS
<ul><li>4 cups brussels sprouts, coarsely chopped, tough centers discarded</li><li>1 cup buttermilk</li><li>1 tsp. Mustard</li><li>3 tbsp. Oil</li><li>½ tsp. Salt</li><li>1 tsp. Onion powder</li><li>1 tsp. Minced garlic flakes</li><li>1 tsp. Dried dill</li><li>1 tsp. Dried parsley</li><li>1 tsp. Celery salt</li></ul>	1. Place sliced brussels sprouts in a container. Blend the seasonings in another small container. 2. Whisk together buttermilk, mustard and oil. Pour over brussels sprouts. 3. Spray dehydrator tray with nonstick spray and place brussels sprouts on tray. Drizzle with seasonings. Set the dehydrator to 110 degrees F and dehydrate for 8-6 hrs.

PER SERVING			
Calories: 16kcal	Fat: 0.2g	Carbs: 3g	Protein: 1.1g

TEX-MEX GREEN BEANS

PREPARATION TIME	COOKING TIME	SERVING
15 mins	6 hrs	4

INGREDIENTS	DIRECTIONS
<ul><li>5 pounds green beans</li><li>one-third cup melted coconut oil</li><li>1 teaspoon Chili powder</li><li>1 teaspoon Cumin</li><li>half teaspoon Each paprika, onion powder, garlic powder, salt and pepper</li></ul>	1. Blanch green beans in boiling water for several mins. Dry beans. 2. Melt coconut oil in microwave. Mix oil and seasonings in a container. 3. Coast green beans in oil mixture. 4. Place green beans onto dehydrator and dry for 8-6 hrs at 125 degrees F.

PER SERVING			
Calories: 12kcal	Fat: 0.2g	Carbs: 2.4g	Protein: 0.6g

ROOT VEGETABLE MEDLEY

PREPARATION TIME	COOKING TIME	SERVING
15 mins	6 hrs	4

INGREDIENTS	DIRECTIONS
<ul><li>two medium beets</li><li>one sweet potato</li><li>2 medium parsnips</li><li>1 medium celery root</li><li>3 tbsp. Olive oil</li><li>1 ½ tsp. Salt</li><li>1 tsp. Garlic powder</li><li>½ tsp. Oregano</li></ul>Pinch of black pepper	1. Wash, peel and slice vegetables as thinly as possible, preferably with a mandolin. 2. Place vegetables in a container. Mix olive oil with seasonings and pour over vegetables. Toss to coat. 3. Lay vegetables on trays using different trays for different vegetables. Dehydrate at 105 degrees F for at least 8 hrs.

PER SERVING			
Calories: 48kcal	**Fat:** 0.2g	**Carbs:** 11g	**Protein:** 1.3g

VEGAN BROCCOLI CRISPS

PREPARATION TIME	COOKING TIME	SERVING
15 mins	6 hrs	4

INGREDIENTS	DIRECTIONS
<ul><li>2 heads broccoli, washed and cut into bite size florets</li><li>½ cup cashews, soaked for at least 1 hour and drained</li><li>4 tbsp. Nutritional yeast</li><li>1 tsp. Curry powder</li><li>½ tsp. red pepper flakes</li></ul>	1. Blend the cashews, nutritional yeast and spices in a food processor. Add water to achieve a smooth texture. Cashews should be fully blended. 2. Pour dressing into a container and add broccoli. Coat the florets evenly. 3. Place florets onto dehydrator sheets and dehydrate at 110 degrees F for 18 hrs.

PER SERVING			
Calories: 104kcal	**Fat:** 6.8g	**Carbs:** 8g	**Protein:** 5.1g

CHAPTER 2: Recipes for Fruits

BANANA COCOA LEATHER

PREPARATION TIME	COOKING TIME	SERVING
30 mins	8 to 10 hrs	6

INGREDIENTS	DIRECTIONS
• four bananas • two tbsps. cocoa powder • one to two tablespoons. corn syrup • 1 teaspoon lemon juice	1. Puree all ingredients until smooth. 2. Pour mixture onto dehydrator trays and spread to ¼ inch thickness. Dehydrate at 130-degree F for 8-10 hrs. About half way through, flip leather to the other side.

PER SERVING			
Calories: 42kcal	**Fat:** 0.8g	**Carbs:** 11g	**Protein:** 1.1g

PLUM FRUIT LEATHER

PREPARATION TIME	COOKING TIME	SERVING
30 mins	8 hrs and 20 mins	12

INGREDIENTS	DIRECTIONS
• 6 purple or red plums split and pitted • 2 tablespoons lemon juice • 2 teaspoons ground cinnamon quarter cup water	1. Put the plums and water inside a pot and simmer until the plums begin to break down, about 10 to 15 mins. 2. When the plums are soft, pour into a mixer and mix till uniform. include lemon juice and cinnamon and blend. 3. Place ParaFlexx Screens on the racks of your dehydrator and set to 140 deg. F. 4. Pour the puree onto the screens and utilize a spoon to spread the puree uniformly, about 1/8 inch thick. 5. Dehydrate for 8 hrs. Make sure the leather is entirely dehydrated and not sticky before removing from the screens.

PER SERVING			
Calories: 31kcal	**Fat:** 0g	**Carbs:** 7g	**Protein:** 0g

GOJI BERRY LEATHER

PREPARATION TIME	COOKING TIME	SERVING
1 hour and 15 mins	7 hrs	2

INGREDIENTS	DIRECTIONS
• one cup dried goji berries • two cups unsweetened applesauce • two tablespoons honey	1. Place goji berries in 1 cup of water and let soak until they are rehydrated, about 1 hour. 2. Pour berries, soaking water, applesauce and honey into the blender and blend until smooth. Add more water if necessary. 3. Spread onto dehydrator sheets and dry at 135 degrees F for 6-7 hrs.

PER SERVING			
Calories: 64kcal	**Fat:** 0.8g	**Carbs:** 14g	**Protein:** 0.5g

STRAWBERRY PASSION FRUIT LEATHER

PREPARATION TIME	COOKING TIME	SERVING
20 mins	6 hrs and 10 mins	6

INGREDIENTS	DIRECTIONS
• two cups fresh strawberries, stems removed • 2 tablespoons passion fruit syrup • 1 cup applesauce	1. Place the strawberries, passion fruit syrup, and applesauce into a blender and puree until smooth. 2. Place ParaFlexx Screens on the racks of your Food Dehydrator and pour the puree onto the screens. 3. Use spatula to distribute the puree so it is about 1/8-inch think evenly. 4. Set your food dehydrator to 140 deg. F and dehydrate for 6 hrs. 5. Make sure your leather is wholly dehydrated and not sticky before removing from the screens.

PER SERVING

Calories: 45kcal	Fat: 0g	Carbs: 12g	Protein: 0g

NOTHING BUT FRUIT BARS

PREPARATION TIME	COOKING TIME	SERVING
30 mins	18 hrs	8

INGREDIENTS	DIRECTIONS
<ul><li>2 cups sprouted buckwheat or quinoa</li><li>1 cup dates</li><li>1 cup dried apricots</li><li>1 tablespoon cinnamon</li><li>1/8 teaspoon cardamom</li><li>1 pear or apple, peeled, cored and diced</li></ul>	1. Place all ingredients in a blender. Blend until smooth. 2. Spread the mixture onto dehydrator trays. Use a spatula to smooth. Dehydrate for 18 hrs at 130 degrees F.

PER SERVING

Calories: 98kcal	Fat: 1.6g	Carbs: 17.6g	Protein: 3.6g

PEACH COBBLER

PREPARATION TIME	COOKING TIME	SERVING
10 mins	8 hrs	4

INGREDIENTS	DIRECTIONS
<ul><li>two peaches, sliced into 1/4 inch slices</li><li>1/3 cup bread crumbs</li><li>1 tablespoon sugar</li><li>1/2 teaspoon cinnamon</li><li>1/2 teaspoon nutmeg</li><li>1/2 cup water</li></ul>	1. Put the peach slices on the rack of your Food dehydrator and set to 125 deg. F. Dehydrate for eight hrs. 2. Remove peach slices from the racks and combine with the breadcrumbs, sugar, cinnamon, and nutmeg. Store in a zipper lock bag until ready to use. 3. To rehydrate, simply combine the contents of the bag with 1/2 cup boiling water and stir.

PER SERVING

Calories: 78kcal	Fat: 0.8g	Carbs: 16.9g	Protein: 1.9g

FRUIT DRIZZLES

PREPARATION TIME	COOKING TIME	SERVING
20 mins	6 to 8 hrs	6 to 8

INGREDIENTS	DIRECTIONS
<ul><li>one cup raspberries or strawberries, hulled</li><li>1 tablespoon sugar</li><li>1 tablespoon orange juice</li><li>Zest of 2 lemons Zest of 2 oranges</li></ul>	1. Dice strawberries and raspberries into small pieces. 2. Combine with sugar, juice and lemon and orange zest. 3. Spread mixture on dehydrator sheets. 4. Dehydrate for 6-8 hrs at 118 degrees F. At this point, fruit should be thoroughly dried. 5. Place all the mixture in a spice grinder and pulse several times until you have drizzles. Top your favorite treats with fruit drizzles for added flavor and color.

PER SERVING			
Calories: 25kcal	Fat: 0g	Carbs: 6.5g	Protein: 0.1g

ASIAN PEAR AND GINGER TREATS

PREPARATION TIME	COOKING TIME	SERVING
20 mins	6 to 12 hrs	6 to 8

INGREDIENTS	DIRECTIONS
<ul><li>6 medium sized Asian pears, peeled, pitted and cored</li><li>1 ½ teaspoon honey</li><li>4 tablespoon warm water</li><li>1 small knob of ginger, finely grated</li></ul>	1. Inside a container, combine honey and ginger. Add the water and mix well. 2. Slice Asian pears into uniform slices, around ¼ inch thick. Arrange pear slices onto dehydrator tray and brush with a thin layer of ginger-honey mixture. 3. Dehydrate for 9-12 hrs at 135 degrees F.

PER SERVING			
Calories: 18kcal	Fat: 0g	Carbs: 4.9g	Protein: 0.1g

TASTY PINEAPPLE CHUNKS

PREPARATION TIME	COOKING TIME	SERVING
10 mins	12 hrs	4

INGREDIENTS	DIRECTIONS
• 1 ripe pineapple	1. Peel and cut pineapple. Cut in 1/2 then cut each half in ¼ inch thick chunks. 2. Place pineapple chunks on dehydrator racks and dehydrate at 135 deg. F for 12 hrs.

PER SERVING			
Calories: 62kcal	Fat: 0.2g	Carbs: 16.2g	Protein: 0.7g

BANANA BREAD PUDDING

PREPARATION TIME	COOKING TIME	SERVING
10 mins	8 hrs	4

INGREDIENTS	DIRECTIONS
• 2 bananas, sliced into rounds • 1/4 cup cashews, chopped • 1/2 cup white bread, cut into large chunks • 1 tablespoon brown sugar	1. Preheat your food dehydrator to 125 deg. F and arrange the banana slices on the racks. Dehydrate for eight hrs, or until everything is totally dried up. 2. Place the bananas and brown sugar in a bag that can be sealed with a zipper. Mix the bread chunks and cashews together in a separate bag that has a zipper lock. 3. To rehydrate, mix together all of the ingredients with a half cup of warm water, then let the mixture lie undisturbed for five mins before combining and serving.

PER SERVING			
Calories: 122kcal	Fat: 4.3g	Carbs: 20.7g	Protein: 2.3g

APPLE FIG FRUIT LEATHER

PREPARATION TIME	COOKING TIME	SERVING
30 mins	8 hrs	6

INGREDIENTS	DIRECTIONS
• 10 figs, ripe and washed • 2 apples, cored and peeled • 1 cup orange juice	1. Boil all ingredients in a covered pot. 2. Simmer fruits for 30 mins. 3. Mix all ingredients using a blender. 4. Place mixture on the dehydrator. 5. Dry for 8 hrs at 125 deg. F.

PER SERVING			
Calories: 104kcal	Fat: 0g	Carbs: 27g	Protein: 1g

PEACH & RASPBERRY

PREPARATION TIME	COOKING TIME	SERVING
15 mins	8 to 10 hrs	6

INGREDIENTS	DIRECTIONS
• 10 Peaches, cut • 3 cup Raspberries • Honey, to taste	1. Puree the peaches into your blender, add honey and transfer to a container. 2. Spread the mixture over dehydrator trays lined with parchment paper. 3. Add the raspberries to the blender then blend until smooth. Pour this mixture over and swirl into the peach mixture. 4. Dehydrate at 120 deg. F for 8-10 hrs. 5. When done, remove from the parchment paper, cut into strips, roll them up in parchment paper and store in airtight containers.

PER SERVING			
Calories: 100.4kcal	Fat: 0.8g	Carbs: 25.2g	Protein: 1.7g

MANGO LIME FRUIT LEATHER

PREPARATION TIME	COOKING TIME	SERVING
15 mins	6 to 9 hrs or more	6

INGREDIENTS	DIRECTIONS
<ul><li>8 Mangos, peeled and diced</li><li>2 Limes, juiced and zested</li><li>Honey, to taste</li></ul>	1. Add the mangoes, lime juice and zest to your blender and blend until pureed. Mix in honey and set aside. 2. Line dehydrator trays with parchment paper then spread the fruit mixture onto it. 3. Dehydrate at 120 deg. F for 6-9 hrs. When done, cut into strips, roll up in parchment paper and store in airtight containers Fruit Leather

PER SERVING

Calories: 141.3kcal	Fat: 0.6g	Carbs: 37.4g	Protein: 1.2g

CHAPTER 3: Recipes for Meat

CHICKEN JERKY

PREPARATION TIME	COOKING TIME	SERVING
10 mins	7 hrs	4

INGREDIENTS	DIRECTIONS
<ul><li>1 ½ lb. chicken tenders, boneless, skinless and cut into ¼ inch strips</li><li>¼ tsp ground ginger</li><li>¼ teaspoon black pepper</li><li>half teaspoon garlic powder</li><li>one tsp lemon juice</li><li>½ cup soy sauce</li></ul>	1. Mix all ingredients except chicken into the zip-lock bag. 2. Add chicken and seal bag and mix until chicken is well coated. Place in refrigerator for 30 mins. 3. Arrange marinated meat slices of dehydrator trays and dehydrate at 145 deg. F for 6-7 hrs.

PER SERVING			
Calories: 342kcal	Fat: 12.6g	Carbs: 2.9g	Protein: 51.3g

BEEF BULGOGI JERKY

PREPARATION TIME	COOKING TIME	SERVING
12hrs and 10 mins	6 hrs	4

INGREDIENTS	DIRECTIONS
<ul><li>two lb. Beef round, sliced</li><li>4 tablespoons brown sugar</li><li>4 tablespoons soy sauce</li><li>1 tablespoon garlic powder</li><li>1 tablespoon sesame oil</li><li>Sal to taste</li></ul>	1. Place the beef inside a sealable plastic bag. 2. Combine all of the remaining components in a container. 3. Include the mixture to the plastic bag. 4. Put the beef in the refrigerator for 12 hrs. 5. Pour the marinade down the drain. 6. Add the beef to the food dehydrator. 7. Set at 165 degrees F. 8. Process for 6 hrs. 9. Storage suggestions: place in a glass jar with lid and store in a cool, dry place.

PER SERVING			
Calories: 307kcal	Fat: 3g	Carbs: 15g	Protein: 8g

MUSTARD BEEF JERKY WITH BALSAMIC VINEGAR

PREPARATION TIME	COOKING TIME	SERVING
12hrs and 10 mins	6 hrs	4

INGREDIENTS	DIRECTIONS
<ul><li>2 lbs. Beef round, cut</li><li>two tbsps. olive oil</li><li>one tbsp. Dijon mustard</li><li>one cup balsamic vinegar</li><li>two garlic cloves, crushed</li><li>one teaspoon salt</li></ul>	1. Add the beef to a sealable plastic bag. 2. Combine the remaining components in a container. 3. Combine thoroughly. 4. Put the solution into the plastic bag. 5. Place in the refrigerator for 12 hrs. 6. Drain the marinade. 7. Add the beef slices to the food dehydrator. 8. Set the dehydrator to 165 degrees F. 9. Dry for 6 hrs. 10. Keep the beef jerky slices in a glass container with lid. Store in an area away from sunlight.

PER SERVING			
Calories: 372kcal	Fat: 27.5g	Carbs: 9.6g	Protein: 24g

RANCH BEEF JERKY

PREPARATION TIME	COOKING TIME	SERVING
15 mins	8 hrs	6

INGREDIENTS	DIRECTIONS
<ul><li>two lbs. flank steak that is cut into thin slices</li><li>¼ tsp cayenne pepper</li><li>1 ½ tsp liquid smoke</li><li>2 tbsps. red pepper flakes</li><li>3 tbsps. ranch seasoning</li><li>¾ cup Worcestershire sauce</li><li>¾ cup soy sauce</li></ul>	1. Add all ingredients into the huge mixing container and mix well. Cover container and place in refrigerator for overnight. 2. Arrange marinated meat slices on dehydrator racks and dehydrate at 145 deg. F for 7-8 hrs.

PER SERVING			
Calories: 346kcal	Fat: 12.9g	Carbs: 9.5g	Protein: 44.3g

PAPRIKA PORK JERKY

PREPARATION TIME	COOKING TIME	SERVING
12 hrs and 10 mins	6 hrs	2

INGREDIENTS	DIRECTIONS
<ul><li>one lb. Pork tenderloin, sliced</li><li>½ cup ketchup</li><li>one tsp. onion powder</li><li>one tsp. garlic powder</li><li>one tsp. smoked paprika</li><li>one tsp. ground mustard</li><li>one tsp. chili powder</li><li>Salt and pepper to taste</li></ul>	1. Add the ketchup to a container. 2. Stir in the onion powder, garlic powder, paprika, mustard, chili powder, salt and pepper. 3. Combine thoroughly. 4. Pour the solution to a sealable plastic bag. 5. Include the pork to the plastic bag. 6. Enclose and put in the fridge for 12 hrs. 7. Remove the pork from the marinade. 8. Add to the food dehydrator. 9. Dry at 158 degrees F for 6 hrs. 10. Store the pork jerky in a glass jar with lid. Store in a cool dry place for up to 2 weeks.

PER SERVING

Calories: 382kcal	Fat: 1.2g	Carbs: 67.1g	Protein: 26.1g

TURKEY JERKY

PREPARATION TIME	COOKING TIME	SERVING
15 mins	5 hrs	4

INGREDIENTS	DIRECTIONS
<ul><li>one pound turkey meat, sliced into fine slices</li><li>one tsp salt</li><li>2 tsp garlic powder</li><li>1 tbsp. onion powder</li><li>2 tsp brown sugar</li><li>1/3 cup Worcestershire sauce</li><li>¼ tsp Tabasco sauce</li><li>2 tbsps. soy sauce</li><li>1 tbsp. liquid smoke</li></ul>	1. Add all ingredients except meat in the large zip-lock bag and mix until well combined. 2. Add meat in bag. Seal bag and massage gently to cover the meat with marinade. Place in refrigerator for overnight. 3. Arrange marinated meat slices on the dehydrator racks and dehydrate at 160 deg. F for 5 hrs.

PER SERVING

Calories: 233kcal	Fat: 5.7g	Carbs: 8.5g	Protein: 34.1g

SWEET & SPICY BEEF JERKY

PREPARATION TIME	COOKING TIME	SERVING
15 mins	6 hrs	8

INGREDIENTS	DIRECTIONS
• two pounds flank steak, clipped fat and cut into fine strips • 1 tsp red pepper flakes • 1 tsp liquid smoke • 1 tsp garlic powder • 1 tsp onion powder • 2 tsp black pepper • 1 tbsp. brown sugar • two-third cup soy sauce • two-third cup Worcestershire sauce	1. Add red pepper flakes, liquid smoke, garlic powder, onion powder, black pepper, brown sugar, soy sauce, and Worcestershire sauce in a large zip-lock bag and mix well. 2. Add sliced meat in the zip-lock bag. Seal the bag well and toss till meat is thoroughly covered. Put in refrigerator for overnight. 3. Arrange marinated meat slices on dehydrator rack and dehydrate at 160 deg. F for 5-6 hrs. 4. Store in air-tight container.

PER SERVING

Calories: 260kcal	Fat: 9.5g	Carbs: 7.7g	Protein: 33.1g

PORK JERKY IN CHIPOTLE SAUCE

PREPARATION TIME	COOKING TIME	SERVING
12 hrs and 10 mins	6 hrs	2

INGREDIENTS	DIRECTIONS
• one tablespoon tomato paste • 7 oz. Chipotle adobo sauce • one teaspoon salt • one tsp. sugar • one tsp. garlic powder • one lb. Pork tenderloin, sliced	1. Mix the tomato paste, chipotle adobo sauce, salt, sugar and garlic powder in a container. 2. Transfer to a sealable plastic bag along with the pork tenderloin slices. 3. Seal and refrigerate for 12 hrs. 4. Drain the marinade. 5. Add the pork slices to the food dehydrator. 6. Process at 158 degrees F for 6 hrs.

7. Storage suggestions: place in a glass jar with lid. Store in a cool dry place, away from sunlight.

PER SERVING			
Calories: 54kcal	**Fat:** 0.3g	**Carbs:** 11.3g	**Protein:** 2.5g

EASY MEXICAN JERKY

PREPARATION TIME	COOKING TIME	SERVING
15 mins	5 hrs	4

INGREDIENTS	DIRECTIONS
<ul><li>1 lb. pork lean meat, sliced thinly</li><li>1 tsp paprika</li><li>½ tsp oregano</li><li>½ tsp garlic powder</li><li>1 tsp chili powder</li><li>¼ tsp black pepper</li><li>1 tsp salt</li></ul>	1. Add paprika, oregano, garlic powder, chili powder, black pepper, and salt inside a container and combine thoroughly. 2. Add sliced meat inside a container and mix until well coated. Cover container and place in refrigerator for overnight. 3. Arrange marinated meat slices on dehydrator rack and dehydrate at 160 deg. F for 5 hrs.

PER SERVING			
Calories: 168kcal	**Fat:** 4.2g	**Carbs:** 1.1g	**Protein:** 29.9g

PERFECT LAMB JERKY

PREPARATION TIME	COOKING TIME	SERVING
10 mins	6 hrs	6

INGREDIENTS	DIRECTIONS
<ul><li>2 ½ lbs. boneless lamb, trimmed fat and slice into thin strips</li><li>½ tsp black pepper</li><li>1 tbsp. oregano</li><li>1 tsp garlic powder</li><li>1 ½ tsp onion powder</li><li>3 tbsps. Worcestershire sauce</li></ul>	1. Add soy sauce, Worcestershire sauce, onion powder, garlic powder, oregano, and black pepper in the big container and mix thoroughly. 2. Include meat slices in the container and combine until thoroughly coated. Cover container tightly and place in refrigerator for overnight.

• 1/3 cup soy sauce	3. Arrange marinated meat slices on dehydrator racks and dehydrate to 145 deg. F for 5-6 hrs.

PER SERVING			
Calories: 373kcal	Fat: 14g	Carbs: 4g	Protein: 54.2g

BEEF JERKY

PREPARATION TIME	COOKING TIME	SERVING
30 mins	4 hrs	4

INGREDIENTS	DIRECTIONS
• two lbs. London broil, sliced thinly • 1 teaspoon sesame oil • three-quarter teaspoon garlic powder • one teaspoon onion powder • 3 tbsps. Brown sugar • 3 tbsps. Soy sauce	1. Add all ingredients except meat in the large zip-lock bag and mix until well combined. 2. Add meat in bag. Seal bag and massage gently to cover the meat with marinade. 3. Let marinate the meat for thirty mins. 4. Arrange marinated meat slices in a single layer on the dehydrator racks and dehydrate at 160 deg. F for 4 hrs.

PER SERVING			
Calories: 347kcal	Fat: 11.2g	Carbs: 8.4g	Protein: 51.1g

FLAVORFUL TERIYAKI JERKY

PREPARATION TIME	COOKING TIME	SERVING
15 mins	6 hrs	6

INGREDIENTS	DIRECTIONS
• 1 ½ lbs. beef bottom round thin meat • 1 tsp onion powder • 1 tsp garlic, minced • 1 tsp red pepper flakes • 1/3 cup soy sauce • 1/3 cup Worcestershire sauce • 1 tsp liquid smoke • ½ cup teriyaki sauce	1. Cut meat into the thin slices. 2. Add teriyaki sauce, onion powder, garlic, red pepper flakes, soy sauce, Worcestershire sauce, and liquid smoke in the large container. 3. Add meat slices in the container and mix until well coated. Cover container tightly and place in refrigerator for overnight. 4. Place marinated meat slices on dehydrator trays and dehydrate at 160 degrees F for 5-6 hrs.

5. Store in air-tight container.

PER SERVING			
Calories: 246kcal	**Fat:** 7.4g	**Carbs:** 8.1g	**Protein:** 33.9g

ASIAN PORK JERKY

PREPARATION TIME	COOKING TIME	SERVING
15 mins	4 hrs 30 mins	6

INGREDIENTS	DIRECTIONS
• 1 lb. pork loin, cut into thin slices • ¼ tsp salt • 1 tsp black pepper • ½ tsp onion powder • ½ tsp garlic powder • 1 tsp sesame oil • 1 tbsp. chili garlic sauce • one tablespoon brown sugar • one tbsp. Worcestershire sauce • one-third cup soy sauce	1. Add all ingredients except meat slices into the large container and mix well. 2. Add sliced meat in the container and mix until well coated. Cover container and place in refrigerator for overnight. 3. Arrange marinated meat slices on the dehydrator racks and dehydrate at 160 deg. F for 4 1/2 hrs.

PER SERVING			
Calories: 249kcal	**Fat:** 13.6g	**Carbs:** 4.3g	**Protein:** 26g

FLAVORFUL TURKEY JERKY

PREPARATION TIME	COOKING TIME	SERVING
15 mins	6 hrs	4

INGREDIENTS	DIRECTIONS
• one pound turkey tenderloins, clipped fat & cut ¼ inch thick • ½ tsp liquid smoke • one teaspoon black pepper • 2 tbsps. brown sugar • two tsp Worcestershire sauce • ¼ cup soy sauce • ½ cup water	1. In a large mixing container, combine together onion powder, liquid smoke, pepper, sugar, Worcestershire sauce, soy sauce, water, and garlic powder. Stir until seasoning dissolve. 2. Add meat slices and mix until well coated. Cover container tightly and refrigerate for overnight. 3. Spray dehydrator racks with cooking spray.

- ¼ tsp garlic powder
- ¼ tsp onion powder

4. Remove marinated meat slices from marinade and shake off excess liquid. Arrange meat slices on dehydrator racks.
5. Arrange dehydrator tray according to the manufacturer's instructions and dry at 145 deg. F for 5-6 hrs.
6. Let cool jerky for 5-10 mins then store in container.

PER SERVING			
Calories: 151kcal	Fat: 1.5g	Carbs: 6.7g	Protein: 29.2g

HICKORY SMOKED JERKY

PREPARATION TIME	COOKING TIME	SERVING
12 hrs and 10 mins	4 hrs	4

INGREDIENTS	DIRECTIONS
<ul><li>one lb. Beef round, sliced</li><li>½ cup hickory smoked marinade</li><li>¼ cup barbecue sauce</li><li>two tbsps. brown sugar</li><li>one tsp. onion powder</li><li>Pinch cayenne pepper</li><li>Salt and pepper, as required</li></ul>	1. Place the beef slices in a sealable plastic bag. 2. Inside a container, mix the marinade, barbecue sauce, sugar, onion powder, cayenne, salt and pepper. 3. Put the solution into the bag. 4. Seal and marinate in the refrigerator for twelve hrs. 5. Discard the marinade and add the beef to the food dehydrator. 6. Process at 180 degrees F for 4 hrs, flipping halfway through. 7. Storage suggestions: store in a glass jar with cover for around two weeks. **Tip**: arrange the meat in a single layer without overlapping.

PER SERVING			
Calories: 238kcal	Fat: 6.1g	Carbs: 20g	Protein: 42g

VENISON JERKY

PREPARATION TIME	COOKING TIME	SERVING
1 day and 30 mins	4 hrs	2

INGREDIENTS	DIRECTIONS
<ul><li>1 lb. Venison roast, silver skin trimmed and sliced thinly</li><li>4 tablespoons coconut amino</li><li>¼ tsp. onion powder</li><li>quarter tsp. garlic powder</li><li>quarter tsp. red pepper flakes</li><li>one tablespoon honey</li><li>4 tbsps. Worcestershire sauce</li><li>Salt and pepper, as required</li></ul>	1. Place the venison roast slices inside a container. 2. In second mixing container, mix the remaining components. 3. Put this solution into the first container. 4. Stir to coat meat evenly with the mixture. 5. Cover the container. 6. Chill in the refrigerator for 1 day, stirring every 3 or 4 hrs. 7. Drain the marinade. 8. Place the venison slices in the food dehydrator. 9. Process at 160 degrees F for 4 hrs. 10. Storage suggestions: store in vacuum sealed bags for up to 3 months or in Ziplock bags for up to 2 weeks. **Tip**: freeze the venison meat for 1 hour before slicing.

PER SERVING			
Calories: 389kcal	**Fat:** 6.4g	**Carbs:** 22.9g	**Protein:** 49.3g

BEER BEEF JERKY

PREPARATION TIME	COOKING TIME	SERVING
6 hrs and 10 mins	5 hrs	2

INGREDIENTS	DIRECTIONS
<ul><li>one lb. Beef round, sliced</li><li>½ cup soy sauce</li><li>two cloves garlic, crushed</li><li>two cups beer</li><li>one tbsp. liquid smoke</li><li>one tbsp. Honey</li><li>Pepper, as required</li></ul>	1. Include the beef to a sealable plastic bag. 2. Combine the rest of the ingredients in a container. 3. Pour the mixture into the bag. 4. Seal and refrigerate for 6 hrs. 5. Drain the marinade. 6. Put the beef in the food dehydrator. 7. Dehydrate at 160 degrees F for 1 hour. 8. Reduce temperature to 150 degrees F and process for additional 4 hrs. 9. Storage suggestions: store in a food container with lid for up to 2 weeks.

PER SERVING

Calories: 389kcal	Fat: 8.5g	Carbs: 31g	Protein: 46g

BUFFALO JERKY

PREPARATION TIME	COOKING TIME	SERVING
15 hrs and 10 mins	6 hrs	4

INGREDIENTS	DIRECTIONS
<ul><li>two lb. Beef round, sliced</li><li>1 teaspoon salt</li><li>1 cup buffalo sauce</li></ul>	1. Season the beef slices with the salt. 2. Add the buffalo sauce to a container. 3. Stir in the seasoned beef. 4. Cover the container. 5. Refrigerate for 15 hrs. 6. Drain the marinade. 7. Add the beef slices to the food dehydrator. 8. Process at 165 degrees F for 6 hrs. 9. Storage suggestions: place the beef jerky in a sealable glass container. Store for around two weeks.

PER SERVING

Calories: 335kcal	Fat: 3g	Carbs: 13g	Protein: 15g

BARBECUE BEEF JERKY

PREPARATION TIME	COOKING TIME	SERVING
12 hrs and 10 mins	6 hrs	4

INGREDIENTS	DIRECTIONS
<ul><li>2 lb. Beef round, sliced</li><li>Salt and pepper to taste</li><li>2 teaspoons dried oregano</li><li>2 teaspoons ground cumin</li><li>1 teaspoon onion powder</li><li>1 teaspoon ground coriander</li><li>4 cloves garlic, grated</li><li>½ cup olive oil</li><li>½ cup lime juice</li><li>1 teaspoon red pepper flakes</li></ul>	1. Add the beef slices to a sealable plastic bag. 2. In a container, mix the salt, pepper, herbs, spices, garlic, olive oil, lime juice and red pepper flakes. 3. Pour mixture into the plastic bag. 4. Turn to coat beef slices evenly with the mixture. 5. Seal and marinate for 12 hrs. 6. Drain the marinade. 7. Put the beef slices to the food dehydrator. 8. Set it to 165 degrees F and process for 6 hrs. 9. Storage suggestions: keep the beef jerky in a vacuum sealed plastic bag.

PER SERVING

Calories: 246kcal	Fat: 4g	Carbs: 25g	Protein: 19g

CHAPTER 4: Recipes for Fish

FISH TERIYAKI JERKY

PREPARATION TIME	COOKING TIME	SERVING
4 hrs and 10 mins	8 hrs	2

INGREDIENTS	DIRECTIONS
• 1 lb. Salmon, sliced • ¼ teaspoon ginger, grated • ¼ cup sugar • ½ cup soy sauce • quarter cup orange juice • one clove garlic, minced	1. Put all of the components into a container and mix them together. 2. Mix well. 3. Transmit to a sealable plastic bag. 4. Seal and refrigerate for four hrs. 5. Drain the marinade. 6. Add the salmon to the food dehydrator. 7. Process at 145 degrees F for 8 hrs. 8. Storage suggestions: store the salmon jerky in a glass jar with lid. **Tip:** you can process longer in the dehydrator if you want the fish slices crispier and dryer..

PER SERVING			
Calories: 389kcal	**Fat:** 6.4g	**Carbs:** 22.9g	**Protein:** 49.3g

SWEET & SMOKY SALMON JERKY

PREPARATION TIME	COOKING TIME	SERVING
15 mins	5 hrs	6

INGREDIENTS	DIRECTIONS
• two lbs. salmon, sliced in strips • 3 tsp black pepper • 3 tbsps. smoked sea salt • ¼ cup liquid smoke • 2 tbsps. black pepper • one cup brown sugar • one cup soy sauce • 1 orange juice	1. Add all ingredients except salmon slices into the large container and mix well. 2. Add sliced salmon in the container and mix until well coated. Cover container and place in refrigerator for overnight. 3. Arrange marinated salmon slices inside a uniform layer on the dehydrator racks and dehydrate at 160 deg. F for 5 hrs

PER SERVING

Calories: 329kcal	Fat: 9.5g	Carbs: 30.5g	Protein: 32.5g

LEMON SALMON JERKY

PREPARATION TIME	COOKING TIME	SERVING
15 mins	4 hrs	6

INGREDIENTS	DIRECTIONS
<ul><li>1 ¼ lbs. salmon, cut into ¼ inch slices</li><li>1/2 tsp liquid smoke</li><li>one and a quarter teaspoon black pepper</li><li>one and a half tbsps. fresh lemon juice</li><li>1 tablespoon molasses</li><li>½ cup soy sauce, low sodium</li></ul>	1. Inside a container, combine together liquid smoke, black pepper, lemon juice, molasses, and soy sauce. 2. Add sliced salmon into the container and mix until well coated. Cover container and place in refrigerator for overnight. 3. Strain sliced salmon in colander and pat dry with paper towel. 4. Arrange sliced salmon on a dehydrator tray and dehydrate at 145 deg. F for 3-4 hrs.

PER SERVING

Calories: 148kcal	Fat: 5.9g	Carbs: 4.5g	Protein: 19.7g

CAJUN FISH JERKY

PREPARATION TIME	COOKING TIME	SERVING
4 hrs and 10 mins	8 hrs	2

INGREDIENTS	DIRECTIONS
<ul><li>one tsp. garlic powder</li><li>one tsp. paprika</li><li>one tsp. onion powder</li><li>¼ tsp. cayenne pepper</li><li>one tablespoon lemon juice</li><li>Salt and pepper to taste</li><li>1 lb. Cod fillet, sliced</li></ul>	1. Combine the spices, lemon juice, salt and pepper inside a container. 2. Season the fish with this mixture. 3. Transfer the seasoned fish and marinade inside an airtight plastic bag. 4. Marinate in the refrigerator for four hrs. 5. Drain the marinade. 6. Arrange the salmon slices on the food dehydrator. 7. Process at 145 degrees F for 8 hrs.

8. Storage suggestions: store in a vacuum sealed plastic bag or glass jar with lid.

Tip: you could utilize other white fish fillet for this recipe.

PER SERVING			
Calories: 246kcal	Fat: 4g	Carbs: 25g	Protein: 19g

LEMON PEPPER FISH JERKY

PREPARATION TIME	COOKING TIME	SERVING
30 mins, plus 4 hrs to chill	6 to 8 hrs	4

INGREDIENTS	DIRECTIONS
<ul><li>2 pounds whitefish fillets, such as cod, haddock, or sole</li><li>Juice and grated zest of one lemon</li><li>two tablespoons distilled white vinegar</li><li>1 tablespoon freshly ground black pepper</li><li>1 teaspoon sea salt</li><li>1 teaspoon onion powder (here)</li><li>1 tablespoon dried parsley</li></ul>	1. Rinse the fish fillets in cold water. Pat them dry with a paper towel. 2. Slice the fillets into ¼-inch slices across the grain. Refrigerate the fish slices while you make the marinade. 3. In a 2-quart container with a lid, combine the lemon juice and zest, vinegar, pepper, salt, onion powder, and parsley. Mix well. 4. Add the sliced fish to the container. Press down on the fish slices to submerge them in the marinade. Cover the marinade container and refrigerate for 4 hrs. 5. Remove the fish from the marinade and drain in a colander. 6. Arrange the fish strips inside a uniform layer on the dehydrator trays. 7. Dehydrate at 165°F for 6 to 8 hrs. 8. When dried, the fish jerky should be firm and tough and have a mild, fishy flavor. If it smells rancid, discard it, as this is a sign of spoilage. 9. If your dehydrator doesn't get as hot as 165° F, use the highest temperature available to you. After the jerky is finished, place it on a paper-towel-lined baking sheet. Bake it in a preheated 275°F oven for 10 mins to bring the internal temperature

up to 165°F. Remove it from the oven. Use a paper towel to blot the surface of the jerky and remove any excess oil.

10. Cool the fish jerky to room temperature before you package it.

11. Fish jerky stored in a vacuum-sealed bag will last for 2 to 3 weeks at room temperature, 3 to 6 months in the fridge, or almost a year in the freezer.

PER SERVING

Calories: 67kcal	Fat: 0.4g	Carbs: 8g	Protein: 7g

SHRIMP

PREPARATION TIME	COOKING TIME	SERVING
45 mins	6 hrs	4

INGREDIENTS	DIRECTIONS
<ul><li>2 lbs. frozen shrimp, cooked, skinned, & deveined</li><li>Juice and grated zest of one lemon</li><li>one tbsp. olive oil</li><li>2 heads garlic</li><li>one (one-inch) piece of ginger root</li></ul>	1. Thaw the shrimp in the refrigerator. It should still be slightly icy when you work with it. 2. Meanwhile, make the marinade. In a medium container, use a fork to lightly whisk the lemon juice and zest and the olive oil to combine. 3. Separate the cloves from each head of garlic. Peel each clove by crushing the clove with the flat part of a knife and removing the papery skin. Press the garlic cloves through a garlic press, one at a time. Add the crushed garlic to the lemon-olive oil mixture. 4. Peel the ginger with the edge of a spoon. Cut the ginger into fine cubes. Add the ginger to the lemon-olive oil mixture. 5. Place the shrimp in a colander. Wash it with cold water, then drain it. 6. Cut each shrimp in half, crosswise. Then cut each half in half again, lengthwise through the vein channel on the back of the shrimp. (If there are any dark spots, scrape the dark vein out of the shrimp with the tip of your knife and discard the dark piece.)

7. Add the prepared shrimp to the marinade. Stir it to coat all sides of the shrimp. Continue to add the shrimp as each one is cut. Stir the shrimp in the marinade after each addition, until all the shrimp have been added. Let the shrimp sit in the marinade for 10 more mins, then drain it.

8. Arrange the shrimp in a uniform layer on the dehydrator trays.

9. Dehydrate at 145°F for 6 hrs or until the shrimp is fully dried.

10. When dried, the shrimp should be hard and brittle with no moisture inside.

11. Dried shrimp stored in Mylar bags with oxygen absorbers will keep for up to a year at room temperature.

PER SERVING

Calories: 104kcal	Fat: 2g	Carbs: 5g	Protein: 9g

SOY MARINATED SALMON JERKY

PREPARATION TIME	COOKING TIME	SERVING
40 mins	16 hrs	12

INGREDIENTS	DIRECTIONS
• 1 lbs. boneless salmon fillet • Salt and pepper, as required • half cup apple cider vinegar • two tbsps. low-sodium soy sauce • 1 tablespoon fresh lemon juice • 2 teaspoons paprika • ½ teaspoon garlic powder	1. Freeze the salmon for about 30 mins until it is firm. 2. Meanwhile, whisk together the apple cider vinegar, soy sauce, and lemon juice in a mixing container. 3. Add the paprika and garlic powder then stir well. Top the salmon with salt and pepper as required then remove the skin. 4. Slice the salmon into ¼-inch thick strips then place them in a container or glass dish. 5. Pour in the marinade, turning to coat, then cover with plastic and chill for 12 hrs. 6. Drain the salmon slices and place them on paper towels to soak up the extra liquid.

7. Spread the salmon slices on your dehydrator trays in a single layer.
8. Dry for 3 to 4 hrs at 145°F until it is dried but still tender and chewy.
9. Cool the salmon jerky completely then store in airtight containers in a cool, dark location.

PER SERVING			
Calories: 40kcal	**Fat:** 1g	**Carbs:** 5g	**Protein:** 4g

TUNA

PREPARATION TIME	COOKING TIME	SERVING
10 mins	3 to 4 hrs	3

INGREDIENTS	DIRECTIONS
• 3 (5-ounce) cans tuna, packed in water	1. Drain the cans of tuna. (If you have pets, reserve the tuna water for them!) 2. Line the dehydrator trays with fruit leather sheets. 3. Break up the tuna with a fork and spread it out on the lined dehydrator trays. 4. Dehydrate at 145°F for 3 to 4 hrs. 5. When dried, the tuna pieces should be hard and dry. 6. Dried tuna stored in vacuum-sealed glass jars with oxygen absorbers will keep for 1 to 2 years.

PER SERVING			
Calories: 58kcal	**Fat:** 0.3g	**Carbs:** 7g	**Protein:** 9.2g

TROUT JERKY

PREPARATION TIME	COOKING TIME	SERVING
15 mins	4 hrs	4

INGREDIENTS	DIRECTIONS
<ul><li>four tablespoons soy sauce</li><li>one teaspoon olive oil</li><li>1 teaspoon garlic, crushed</li><li>one tbsp. light brown sugar</li><li>half tsp. ground black pepper</li><li>16 ounces trout fillets, cut into 1-inch wide strips lengthwise</li></ul>	1. For marinade: inside a small-sized saucepan, include the entire components excluding for trout strips over medium heat and bring it to a gentle boil, stirring continuously. 2. Transfer the marinade into a container and set aside to cool completely. 3. Place trout strips and marinade into a zip-top bag and shake vigorously to coat. 4. Refrigerate the zip-top bag to marinate for 6 hrs, shaking the bag occasionally. 5. Remove marinated trout from bag and place into a strainer for about 5 mins. 6. With a paper towel, gently pat dry the trout strips. 7. Set the temperature of your dehydrator to 150°F (66°C). 8. Arrange the trout strips onto the dehydrator trays. 9. Dehydrate for approximately 4 hrs, blotting off any fat droplets occasionally. 10. Remove the trout strips from dehydrator and set aside to cool completely. 11. Store jerky in airtight containers for up to 2 weeks or in freezer for 6 months.

PER SERVING			
Calories: 244kcal	**Fat:** 10.8g	**Carbs:** 3.8g	**Protein:** 31.3g

CHAPTER 5: Dehydrated Bread And Chips

GARLIC ZUCCHINI CHIPS

PREPARATION TIME	COOKING TIME	SERVING
15 mins	4 hrs	4

INGREDIENTS	DIRECTIONS
<ul><li>three zucchinis, cut into thin rounds</li><li>two tbsps. olive oil</li><li>two tbsps. sesame seeds</li><li>two tbsps. dried thyme, crushed</li><li>two cloves garlic, grated</li><li>Salt, as required</li></ul>	1. Coat the zucchini with olive oil. 2. Drizzle with the sesame seeds, thyme, garlic and salt. 3. Add these to the food dehydrator. 4. Dehydrate at 158 degrees F for 2 hrs. 5. Flip and dry for another 2 hrs. 6. Storage suggestions: store in a sealable plastic bag. **Tip**: before dehydrating, press the zucchini rounds with paper towel to remove excess moisture.

PER SERVING			
Calories: 70kcal	**Fat:** 4g	**Carbs:** 30g	**Protein:** 2g

BANANA CHIPS

PREPARATION TIME	COOKING TIME	SERVING
15 mins	12 hrs	4

INGREDIENTS	DIRECTIONS
<ul><li>4 bananas, cut thinly</li><li>one tsp. lemon juice</li></ul>	1. Drizzle the banana slices with lemon juice. 2. Add these to the food dehydrator. 3. Process at 135 degrees F for 12 hrs. 4. Storage suggestions: store in a vacuum sealed plastic for up to 3 months. **Tip**: drizzling bananas with lemon juice prevents browning.

PER SERVING			
Calories: 70kcal	**Fat:** 4g	**Carbs:** 30g	**Protein:** 2g

SESAME & CARROT CRACKERS

PREPARATION TIME	COOKING TIME	SERVING
45 mins	24 hrs	15

INGREDIENTS	DIRECTIONS
<ul><li>1 ½ cups of golden flaxseeds</li><li>¼ cup sesame seeds</li><li>2 cups carrot pulp</li><li>one tsp. garlic powder</li><li>half tsp. ground coriander</li><li>3 tablespoons tamari</li><li>1 cup water</li></ul>	1. Grind the flaxseeds in the spice grinder. 2. Add to a container along with the remaining ingredients. 3. Mix well. 4. Let sit for 30 mins. 5. Spread the mixture in the food dehydrator. 6. Process at 110 degrees F for 24 hrs. 7. Storage suggestions: stock inside a sealed jar for around 7 days. **Tip:** make your own garlic powder.

PER SERVING			
Calories: 122kcal	**Fat:** 7.4g	**Carbs:** 10.8g	**Protein:** 3.9g

PEANUT BUTTER & BANANA CRACKERS

PREPARATION TIME	COOKING TIME	SERVING
4 hrs and 20 mins	6 hrs	12

INGREDIENTS	DIRECTIONS
<ul><li>three bananas, sliced</li><li>½ cup peanut butter</li><li>½ teaspoon cinnamon powder</li><li>1 cup ground peanuts</li><li>3 cups graham cracker crumbs</li></ul>	1. Mash the bananas and peanut butter inside a container. 2. Mix in the remaining components. 3. Roll the dough into a large ball. 4. Flatten the ball to form a long rectangle. 5. Wrap the dough with wax paper and refrigerate for 4 hrs. 6. Roll out the dough and slice.

7. Add the slices to the food dehydrator.
8. Process at 145 degrees F for 6 hrs.
9. Storage suggestions: store in a glass jar with cover for around five days.

Tip: do not skip refrigerating the dough before the dehydration process.

PER SERVING			
Calories: 178kcal	Fat: 13.3g	Carbs: 10.7g	Protein: 4.4g

RAW ZUCCHINI BREAD

PREPARATION TIME	COOKING TIME	SERVING
20 mins	6 hrs	6

INGREDIENTS	DIRECTIONS
<ul><li>two cups walnuts</li><li>two teaspoons cinnamon</li><li>one and a half cup dates</li><li>1 teaspoon vanilla extract</li><li>3 cups grated zucchini</li><li>1 cup shredded unsweetened coconut</li><li>1/2 cup raisins</li><li>1/2 cup psyllium husk</li></ul>	1. Add the walnuts to your food processor then pulse until ground. Add the cinnamon, dates, and vanilla and process until combined. 2. Transfer to a container, add the zucchini, coconut, raisins, and psyllium husk and mix well to combine. 3. Use the mixture to make 10 loaves and put them onto the dehydrator trays lined with parchment paper. 4. Dehydrate at 150 deg. F for an hour, reduce the temperature to 110 deg. F and dehydrate for 5 more hrs. 5. When done, allow to cool then store in the fridge.

PER SERVING			
Calories: 373.7kcal	Fat: 22.5g	Carbs: 45.9g	Protein: 6.9g

PUMPKIN CHIPS

PREPARATION TIME	COOKING TIME	SERVING
15 mins	18 hrs and 10 mins	6

INGREDIENTS	DIRECTIONS
<ul><li>one pumpkin</li><li>2 tbsps. coconut oil, melted</li><li>1 tsp. cinnamon</li><li>1 tsp. nutmeg</li></ul>	1. Remove the seeds, pulp, and skin from the pumpkin, and cut the pumpkin flesh into fine slices. 2. Try to make the slices no more than 1/8 inch thick. 3. In a large container, combine the pumpkin slices, coconut oil, cinnamon, nutmeg, and salt. Stir well to coat. 4. Put the pumpkin slices on the stands of your food dehydrator and set to 125 deg. F. Dehydrated for 18 hrs or till the slices are crispy.

PER SERVING			
Calories: 140kcal	Fat: 8g	Carbs: 16g	Protein: 2g

PEAR CHIPS

PREPARATION TIME	COOKING TIME	SERVING
10 mins	6 hrs	10

INGREDIENTS	DIRECTIONS
<ul><li>10 pears, cored and sliced thinly</li></ul>	1. Arrange the pear slices in the food dehydrator. 2. Dehydrate at 145 degrees F for 8 hrs. 3. Storage suggestions: store in a sealed food container for up to 7 days. **Tip**: make sure the pear slices do not overlap to ensure even crisp.

PER SERVING			
Calories: 70kcal	Fat: 4g	Carbs: 30g	Protein: 2g

SEAWEED & TAMARI CRACKERS

PREPARATION TIME	COOKING TIME	SERVING
15 mins	24 hrs	15

INGREDIENTS	DIRECTIONS
<ul><li>1 cup flax seeds</li><li>2 nori sheets, broken</li><li>2 tablespoons tamari</li><li>1 ½ cups water</li></ul>	1. Mix all the ingredients in a container. 2. Spread a layer in the food dehydrator. 3. Set it at 110 degrees F. 4. Process for 24 hrs. 5. Break into crackers. **Tip**: soak flaxseeds in water for 1 hour before processing.

PER SERVING

Calories: 122kcal	Fat: 7.4g	Carbs: 10.8g	Protein: 3.9g

BLACK BREAD

PREPARATION TIME	COOKING TIME	SERVING
30 mins	8 to 12 hrs	4

INGREDIENTS	DIRECTIONS
<ul><li>two garlic cloves, peeled</li><li>quarter cup water</li><li>one teaspoon lemon juice</li><li>quarter cup sliced red onion</li><li>one tbsp. agave nectar</li><li>one tbsp. cacao powder</li><li>quarter cup ground flax seeds</li><li>one tbsp. caraway seeds</li><li>quarter tsp. black pepper</li><li>one cup raw walnuts, soaked overnight, rinsed and drained</li><li>1 cup buckwheat groats, soaked overnight, rinsed and drained</li></ul>	1. Add the walnuts and buckwheat groats to your blender or mixing bowl and beat until chopped. Include the garlic, water, lemon juice, onion, and agave nectar and beat until combined. 2. Transfer to a medium container then mix in the cacao, flaxseed meal, caraway seeds, and pepper. 3. Pour the dough onto a dehydrator sheet, spread it until it is ¼-inch thick and score it into squares or rectangles. 4. Dehydrate at 115 deg. F for 8 to 12 depending on the preferred doneness. 5. When done, break into pieces and store in airtight containers.

PER SERVING

Calories: 324.1kcal	Fat: 18.7g	Carbs: 38.4g	Protein: 9.8g

EGGPLANT CHIPS

PREPARATION TIME	COOKING TIME	SERVING
30 mins	6 hrs and 15 mins	6

INGREDIENTS	DIRECTIONS
• 4 baby eggplants, cut thin • 3 tablespoons olive oil • 1/2 teaspoon smoked paprika • 1/2 teaspoon oregano • 1/4 teaspoon cayenne pepper 2 tablespoons salt	1. Inside a huge container, mix the eggplant slices olive oil, paprika, oregano, cayenne pepper, and salt. 2. Put the eggplant slices on the stands of your food dehydrator and set to 135 deg. F. 3. Dehydrate for 5- 6 hrs or till eggplant slices are entirely dried and crispy.

PER SERVING			
Calories: 35kcal	Fat: 1g	Carbs: 8g	Protein: 1g

GREEN CRACKERS

PREPARATION TIME	COOKING TIME	SERVING
20 mins	8 hrs	4

INGREDIENTS	DIRECTIONS
• 1 cup green juice pulp • ¼ cup ground flax seeds • ¼ cup chia seeds • ¼ cup nutritional yeast • two tbsps. sesame seeds • one tablespoon tamari • ½ tsp. salt • ¼ cup water	1. Mix the entire components inside a container. 2. Transmit to a food processor. 3. Pulse until fully combined. 4. Spread a thin layer of the mixture in the food dehydrator. 5. Score the crackers. 6. Process at 115 degrees F for 5 hrs. 7. Flip the crackers. 8. Dry for another 3 hrs. 9. Storage suggestions: store in a sealable plastic bag for up to 7 days. **Tip**: the mixture layer should be 1/8 inch thick only.

PER SERVING			
Calories: 122kcal	Fat: 7.4g	Carbs: 10.8g	Protein: 3.9g

CRUNCH GREEN BEAN CHIPS

PREPARATION TIME	COOKING TIME	SERVING
15 mins	12 hrs and 10 mins	12

INGREDIENTS	DIRECTIONS
• three lbs. Fresh green beans • 1/4 cup coconut oil, melted • 1 tablespoon salt	1. Combine your green beans and oil and stir well to coat. Season with salt and stir again. 2. Place the green beans on the stands of your food dehydrator and set to 125 deg. F. 3. Dehydrate for 12 hrs or till the beans are dehydrated and crispy. 4. Remove the green beans from the racks and store in a cool dry place.

PER SERVING			
Calories: 130kcal	Fat: 5g	Carbs: 20g	Protein: 2g

SWEET POTATO CHIPS

PREPARATION TIME	COOKING TIME	SERVING
15 mins	14 hrs	6

INGREDIENTS	DIRECTIONS
• 2 large sweet potatoes • 2 teaspoons coconut oil, melted • 2 teaspoons salt	1. Slice the potatoes into thin rounds. Combine your potato slices, salt, and coconut oil and toss to coat. 2. Place ParaFlexx Screens on the racks of your Food Dehydrator and place your potato on the screens in a uniform layer. 3. Set your food dehydrator to 125 deg. F and dehydrate for 12 to 14 hrs or until crisp. Transfer to a tray and store in a cool dry place if not using instantly.

PER SERVING			
Calories: 125kcal	Fat: 10g	Carbs: 9g	Protein: 1g

MEXICAN CRACKERS

PREPARATION TIME	COOKING TIME	SERVING
30 mins	6 hrs	15

INGREDIENTS	DIRECTIONS
<ul><li>½ cup chia seeds</li><li>1 cup golden flaxseeds</li><li>½ cup pumpkin seeds</li><li>½ cup sunflower seeds</li><li>1 red bell pepper, chopped</li><li>¼ onion, chopped</li><li>1 cup carrot pulp</li><li>1 ½ teaspoons chipotle powder</li><li>1 teaspoon garlic powder</li><li>Salt, as required</li><li>½ teaspoon cayenne pepper</li></ul>	1. Inside a blender process all the seeds until powdery. 2. Stir in the bell pepper and onion. 3. Pulse until smooth. 4. Mix in the remaining components. 5. Beat till fully combined. 6. Spread the mixture in the food dehydrator. 7. Score the crackers. 8. Dry at 115 degrees F for 6 hrs. 9. Storage suggestions: store in a sealed food container for up to 5 days. **Tip**: immerse the seeds in separate containers of water for 6 hrs before processing.

PER SERVING			
Calories: 122kcal	**Fat:** 7.4g	**Carbs:** 10.8g	**Protein:** 3.9g

PICKLE CHIPS

PREPARATION TIME	COOKING TIME	SERVING
5 mins	12 hrs	12

INGREDIENTS	DIRECTIONS
<ul><li>one jar big dill pickles</li></ul>	1. Remove pickles from the jar then pat dry with paper towels. Slice the pickles length-wise into long, fine slabs about 1/4 inch thick. 2. Lay the pickle slices on the stands of your dehydrator and set to 125F. Dehydrate for 12 hrs or till the pickles are fully dried. 3. Remove from the racks and eat like chips or store and rehydrate when needed. To rehydrate simply place the dried pickle slices

	in a container of lukewarm water and wait 5 to 10 mins.	

PER SERVING

Calories: 1kcal	Fat: 0g	Carbs: 0.3g	Protein: 0.1g

BEET CHIPS

PREPARATION TIME	COOKING TIME	SERVING
12 hrs	12 hrs	10

INGREDIENTS	DIRECTIONS
• 4 large beets cut into thin rounds • 1 cup apple cider vinegar	1. Inside a wide shallow container or tray, pour the vinegar and organize the beet slices in a uniform layer. Allow the beet slices to soak for 12 hrs. 2. Remove the beets from the vinegar and pat dry with paper towels. 3. Lay the beet slices on the stands of your food dehydrator and set to 125F. Dehydrate for 12 hrs or till beet slices are thoroughly dried. Store in zip-lock bags until ready to use.

PER SERVING

Calories: 23kcal	Fat: 0.1g	Carbs: 4.2g	Protein: 0.7g

POTATO CHIPS

PREPARATION TIME	COOKING TIME	SERVING
10 mins	6 hrs	6

INGREDIENTS	DIRECTIONS
• 2 russet potatoes, skinned • Vegetable oil spray • Salt	1. Wash and peel the potatoes and use a mandolin to slice them into thin rounds. Lay the rounds onto a baking sheet and spray with cooking oil on each ends. 2. Drizzle the rounds with salt and place on the stands of your food dehydrator. Set to

110F and dehydrate for 6 hrs or till the chips are dried and crispy.

3. Store in a large zip-lock bag until ready to use.

PER SERVING			
Calories: 49kcal	Fat: 0.1g	Carbs: 11.2g	Protein: 1.2g

CINNAMON APPLE CHIPS

PREPARATION TIME	COOKING TIME	SERVING
15 mins	12 hrs	4

INGREDIENTS	DIRECTIONS
<ul><li>4 apples, cored, sliced 1/8 inch thick</li><li>1 teaspoon ground cinnamon</li><li>2 cups water</li><li>1 tablespoon lemon juice</li><li>1 tablespoon vinegar</li></ul>	1. In a container, add water, lemon juice, and vinegar and mix well. 2. Add apple slices in the water and let sit for 5 mins. 3. Remove apple slices from water then pat dry with paper towel. 4. Arrange apple slices on a dehydrator tray and drizzle with cinnamon and dehydrate at 135 F/ 58 C for 12 hrs.

PER SERVING			
Calories: 119kcal	Fat: 0.4g	Carbs: 31.4g	Protein: 0.7g

GREEN APPLE CHIPS

PREPARATION TIME	COOKING TIME	SERVING
10 mins	8 hrs	4

INGREDIENTS	DIRECTIONS
<ul><li>4 green apples, cored and sliced 1/8 inch thick</li><li>½ lime juice</li></ul>	1. Add apple slices and lime juice in a container and whisk thoroughly and put away for 5 mins. 2. Arrange apple slices on dehydrator trays and dehydrate at 145 F/ 63 C for 8 hrs. 3. Store in air-tight container.

PER SERVING

Calories: 117kcal	Fat: 0.4g	Carbs: 31.3g	Protein: 0.6g

VEGAN BREAD

PREPARATION TIME	COOKING TIME	SERVING
30 mins	6 hrs	6

INGREDIENTS	DIRECTIONS
<ul><li>one head cauliflower</li><li>one tsp. turmeric</li><li>two tbsps. flax seed</li><li>half cup psyllium husk</li><li>half cup brewer's yeast</li><li>4 large zucchinis</li><li>Salt and black pepper</li></ul>	1. Place cauliflower and zucchini in a food processor and pulse until they form a paste. 2. Add the turmeric, flax seeds, psyllium, yeast, and a tweak of salt and black pepper. 3. Pulse again until all ingredients are thoroughly combined. 4. Place ParaFlexx Screens on the racks of your Food Dehydrator. 5. Form the mixture into slices about 1/2-inch-thick, and place on the screens. 6. Set your food dehydrator to 150F and dehydrate for 6 hrs. 7. The bread should not be dehydrated. One side should be slightly soft.

PER SERVING

Calories: 219kcal	Fat: 1.9g	Carbs: 61.6g	Protein: 10.1g

CHAPTER 6: Recipes for Herbs

DRIED BASIL POWDER

PREPARATION TIME	COOKING TIME	SERVING
10 mins	15 hrs	5

INGREDIENTS	DIRECTIONS
• three cups basil leaves	1. Add the basil leaves to the food dehydrator.
	2. Dry at 105 degrees F for 15 hrs.
	3. Grind the dried basil in a spice grinder or food processor.
	4. Storage suggestions: store in an empty spice jar.
	Tip: use only fresh basil leaves.

PER SERVING			
Calories: 198kcal	**Fat**: 12g	**Carbs**: 16g	**Protein**: 8g

TOMATO POWDER

PREPARATION TIME	COOKING TIME	SERVING
15 mins	12 hrs	5

INGREDIENTS	DIRECTIONS
• Skins from 10 tomatoes	1. Add the tomato skins to a food dehydrator.
	2. Dry at 135 deg. F for 12 hrs.
	3. Transfer the dried tomatoes to a coffee grinder.
	4. Grind until the mixture turns to powder.
	5. Storage suggestions: store in a glass jar with lid.
	Tip: you can also make tomato flakes from this recipe.

PER SERVING			
Calories: 243kcal	**Fat:** 14g	**Carbs:** 25g	**Protein:** 14g

GREEN ONION POWDER

PREPARATION TIME	COOKING TIME	SERVING
10 mins	12 hrs	12

INGREDIENTS	DIRECTIONS
• half pound green onions	1. Add the tomato skins to a food dehydrator.
	2. Dry at 135 deg. F for 12 hrs.
	3. Transfer the dried tomatoes to a coffee grinder.
	4. Grind until the mixture turns to powder.
	5. Storage suggestions: store in a glass jar with lid.

PER SERVING			
Calories: 6kcal	**Fat:** 0g	**Carbs:** 1.4g	**Protein:** 0.4g

LEEK POWDER

PREPARATION TIME	COOKING TIME	SERVING
5 mins	12 hrs	5

INGREDIENTS	DIRECTIONS
• 4 cups leeks, sliced	1. Place the leeks in the food dehydrator.
	2. Dehydrate at 135 degrees F for 4 hrs.
	3. Put the dried leeks in a spice grinder.
	4. Grind until powdery.
	5. Storage suggestions: store in a tightly sealed food or spice container.
	Tip: do not use any browned parts of leeks.

PER SERVING			
Calories: 23kcal	**Fat:** 14g	**Carbs:** 2g	**Protein:** 4g

DRIED HERB MIX

PREPARATION TIME	COOKING TIME	SERVING
15 mins	8 hrs	5

INGREDIENTS	DIRECTIONS
• ½ cup thyme leaves • ½ cup rosemary leaves • two teaspoons lemon zest • 6 cloves garlic, peeled	1. Mix the entire components into a mixing bowl. 2. Pulse till uniform. 3. Spread the mixture in the food dehydrator. 4. Dehydrate at 135 deg. F for 8 hrs. 5. Storage suggestions: store in an empty spice bottle. **Tip**: you can also add other herbs into the mix such as oregano or thyme.

PER SERVING			
Calories: 98kcal	Fat: 12g	Carbs: 16g	Protein: 8g

THYME, GARLIC, ROSEMARY & LEMON HERB MIX

PREPARATION TIME	COOKING TIME	SERVING
15 mins	8 hrs	5

INGREDIENTS	DIRECTIONS
• half cup thyme leaves • 6 cloves garlic, skinned • ½ cup rosemary leaves • 2 teaspoons lemon zest	1. Put the entire components in a mixing bowl. 2. Beat till well mixed. 3. Add the mixture to the food dehydrator. 4. Dry at 135 degrees F for 8 hrs. 5. Storage suggestions: store in a mason jar. **Tip**: you can also use garlic powder in lieu of garlic slices with this recipe.

PER SERVING			
Calories: 43kcal	Fat: 14g	Carbs: 5g	Protein: 14g

LEMON POWDER

PREPARATION TIME	COOKING TIME	SERVING
30 mins	12 hrs	5

INGREDIENTS	DIRECTIONS
• Peel from 6 lemons	1. Add the lemon peels to the food dehydrator. 2. Dehydrate at 95 degrees F for 12 hrs. 3. Transfer to a food processor. 4. Pulse until powdered. 5. Storage suggestions: store in sealable plastic bags. **Tip**: you can stir in garlic powder for lemon garlic mix.

PER SERVING			
Calories: 85kcal	**Fat:** 13g	**Carbs:** 32g	**Protein:** 11g

DRIED PARSLEY, BASIL & OREGANO POWDER

PREPARATION TIME	COOKING TIME	SERVING
15 mins	8 hrs	5

INGREDIENTS	DIRECTIONS
• 2 tablespoons parsley leaves • 2 tablespoons basil leaves • 2 tablespoons oregano leaves • 2 tablespoons brown sugar • 2 tablespoons salt	1. Add the herb leaves to the food dehydrator. 2. Dehydrate at 135 deg. F for 8 hrs. 3. Transfer the dried leaves to a food processor. 4. Stir in the sugar and salt. 5. Storage suggestions: store in a mason jar with lid. **Tip**: you can stir in garlic powder for lemon garlic mix.

PER SERVING			
Calories: 98kcal	**Fat:** 12g	**Carbs:** 16g	**Protein:** 8g

ONION POWDER

PREPARATION TIME	COOKING TIME	SERVING
10 mins	8 hrs	5

INGREDIENTS	DIRECTIONS
• 5 onions, sliced	1. Organize the onion slices in a one layer in the food dehydrator.
	2. Dehydrate at 145 degrees F for 8 hrs.
	3. Transfer the dried onion to a food processor.
	4. Pulse until powdery.
	5. Storage suggestions: store the onion powder in a mason jar.

PER SERVING			
Calories: 76kcal	Fat: 5g	Carbs: 5g	Protein: 3g

PARSLEY, OREGANO, BASIL, THYME & RED PEPPER HERB MIX

PREPARATION TIME	COOKING TIME	SERVING
15 mins	8 hrs	5

INGREDIENTS	DIRECTIONS
• 2 tablespoons fresh oregano leaves	1. Mix the entire components inside a container.
• 2 tablespoons fresh parsley leaves	2. Include to the food dehydrator.
• 2 tablespoons fresh basil leaves	3. Dehydrate at 135 deg. F for 8 hrs.
• 1 tablespoon fresh thyme leaves	4. After dehydrating the herbs and spices, transfer to a food processor.
• 1 teaspoon lemon zest	5. Pulse until powdery.
• 1 teaspoon red pepper, sliced	6. Storage suggestions: store in a glass jar with lid.
	Tip: you can also use red pepper flakes for this recipe.

PER SERVING			
Calories: 15kcal	Fat: 13g	Carbs: 2g	Protein: 1g

GARLIC POWDER

PREPARATION TIME	COOKING TIME	SERVING
15 mins	12 hrs	2

INGREDIENTS	DIRECTIONS
• 6 heads garlic, cloves separated, peeled and sliced	1. Spread the garlic slices in the food dehydrator. 2. Dry at 125 degrees F for 12 hrs. 3. Transfer the dried garlic into a blender or spice grinder. 4. Storage suggestions: sift the mixture before storing. Store the garlic powder in an airtight spice jar. Keep it inside a cool and dry area.

PER SERVING			
Calories: 98kcal	Fat: 2g	Carbs: 16g	Protein: 8g

POWDERED GINGER

PREPARATION TIME	COOKING TIME	SERVING
15 mins	8 hrs	5

INGREDIENTS	DIRECTIONS
• 5 pieces ginger, sliced	1. Put the ginger in the food dehydrator. 2. Dry at 95 deg. F for 8 hrs. 3. Transmit the dried ginger to a food processor or spice grinder. 4. Grind the dried ginger into powder. 5. Storage suggestions: store in a mason jar. **Tip**: use a mandoliner slicer to slice the ginger.

PER SERVING			
Calories: 75kcal	Fat: 3g	Carbs: 5g	Protein: 10g

ONION & GARLIC POWDER MIX

PREPARATION TIME	COOKING TIME	SERVING
20 mins	12 hrs	-

INGREDIENTS	DIRECTIONS
• 5 cloves garlic, skinned & sliced • one onion, sliced	1. Place the garlic and onion slices in the food dehydrator. 2. Dehydrate at 135 degrees F for 12 hrs. 3. Transfer to a spice grinder. 4. Grind until powdery. 5. Storage suggestions: store in a mason jar. **Tip**: slice the onion and garlic thinly before dehydrating.

PER SERVING			
Calories: 75kcal	**Fat:** 3g	**Carbs:** 5g	**Protein:** 10g

HOMEMADE CHILI POWDER

PREPARATION TIME	COOKING TIME	SERVING
15 mins	5 to 6 hrs	24

INGREDIENTS	DIRECTIONS
• 12 red chili peppers	1. Place ParaFlexx Screens on the racks of your Food Dehydrator. 2. Carefully slice the chili peppers into thin strips. Note: The amount of heat in your chili powder will depend on how much pith and seed you allow to stay with the peppers. If you want super-hot powder keep the seeds and pith. For less spicy powder discard most of the seeds and pith. 3. Lay the peppers (and seeds and pith if desired) on the screens and set your Food dehydrator to 115 deg. F. 4. Dehydrate for 5-6 hrs or until the peppers are completely dried. Transfer the contents

of your Food dehydrator to a blender and pulse until a rough powder forms. Store in jars or zipper lock bags.

PER SERVING

Calories: 1kcal	Fat: 0g	Carbs: 0.2g	Protein: 1g

CHAPTER 7: Recipes for Cereals, Nuts, and Seeds

APPLE AND NUT "RAW" CEREAL

PREPARATION TIME	COOKING TIME	SERVING
15 mins	6 hrs	4

INGREDIENTS	DIRECTIONS
• one apple, skinned, cored & diced • 1 cup sprouted wheat berries • ½ cup flax seeds, ground • ½ cup diced raw walnuts • ½ cup millet flour • 1 cup sunflower seeds • 1 tsp. cinnamon • ¼ tsp. salt • ¼ cup coconut oil, melted • ¼ cup maple syrup • 3 tbsp. Apple juice	1. Combine apple, wheat berries, flax seeds, walnuts, flour, seeds, cinnamon and salt. 2. Blend coconut oil, maple syrup and apple juice with a whisk. 3. Add dry ingredients to wet ingredients and stir thoroughly. 4. Dehydrate at 115 degrees F for 18-24 hrs. When crispy, break into large pieces.

PER SERVING			
Calories: 120kcal	Fat: 7.6g	Carbs: 9.9g	Protein: 4.2g

ORANGE-SCENTED GRANOLA WITH DRIED BLUEBERRIES

PREPARATION TIME	COOKING TIME	SERVING
15 mins	6 hrs	4

INGREDIENTS	DIRECTIONS
• 2 cups raw buckwheat or oat groats • 1 cup dates, pitted • 1 cup freshly squeezed orange juice • 1 orange, juiced • 1 tsp. almond extract • 1 tsp. lemon juice • ½ cup dried blueberries	1. Soak the groats in water and drain after about 1 hour. Rinse well and drain again. Transfer them to a small container. 2. In a food processor, pulse all other ingredients except dried blueberries until a paste forms. Blend this mixture with the groats. Mix thoroughly. 3. Spread mixture on dehydrator sheets. Dehydrate for 12 hrs at 115 degrees F and flip over. Dehydrate for another 12-15 hrs until granola is crispy. 4. After dehydrating, crumble granola into bite size pieces and add dried blueberries.

PER SERVING			
Calories: 85kcal	**Fat:** 0.7g	**Carbs:** 17.4g	**Protein:** 2.2g

APPLE CINNAMON GRAHAM COOKIES

PREPARATION TIME	COOKING TIME	SERVING
15 mins	6 hrs	4

INGREDIENTS	DIRECTIONS
• 1 cup cashews, soaked for 1 hour • 1 cup pecans, soaked for 1 hour • 6 cups ground almonds • 2 apples, peeled, cored and chopped • 1 pear, peeled, cored and chopped • 1 cup almond butter • 1 ½ cups flax seed • ½ cup honey • 1 tbsp. Cinnamon	1. After nuts have been soaked, drain and rinse them. 2. Pulse cashews and pecans in food processor until small crumbs form. Add the ground almonds and place in a container. 3. In the food processor, combine apples, pear, almond butter, flax seed, honey, cinnamon, nutmeg and salt. Add the ground nuts. 4. Spread mixture on dehydrator trays, about ¼ inch thick, to the edges.

• ½ tsp. Nutmeg • Pinch of salt	5. Dehydrate 6-8 hrs at 115 degrees F. Flip over and cut into squares. Continue dehydrating for 6-8 hrs or until crunchy.

PER SERVING

Calories: 160kcal	Fat: 13.3g	Carbs: 6.8g	Protein: 5.1g

ALMOND CRANBERRY COOKIES

PREPARATION TIME 15 mins	COOKING TIME 6 hrs	SERVING 4

INGREDIENTS	DIRECTIONS
• Wet pulp from almond milk • 1 banana • 2 tbsp. Coconut oil • ¾ cup shredded coconut flakes • ½ cup dried cranberries • 1 tbsp. Honey • ½ cup almonds, coarsely chopped	1. Place almond pulp, banana and coconut oil in food processor. 2. Mix remainder of ingredients and add to the almond pulp mixture. 3. Place a small scoop of dough on dehydrator sheets and flatten into a cookie. 4. Set temperature to 105 degrees F and dehydrate for 6 hrs or more.

PER SERVING

Calories: 91kcal	Fat: 7.6g	Carbs: 4.8g	Protein: 2g

BANANA BREAKFAST CREPES

PREPARATION TIME 15 mins	COOKING TIME 6 hrs	SERVING 4

INGREDIENTS	DIRECTIONS
• 2 average size ripe bananas • 1 tsp. Ground flax seed • 1 tsp. Almond meal • 1 tsp. Almond milk • Dash of cinnamon	1. Place the entire components inside a food processor afterwards mix into a liquid. 2. Line 2 dehydrator sheets and pour mixture onto them. Liquid should only be about 1/8 inches in thickness. Spread with a spatula.

3. Dehydrate at 115 degrees F for 3 hrs. Crepes should be totally smooth. Do not remove crepes early or they will not hold their shape. Cut into crepe-sized circles.

PER SERVING			
Calories: 48kcal	Fat: 2g	Carbs: 6.6g	Protein: 1.2g

FLAX SEED CRACKERS

PREPARATION TIME	COOKING TIME	SERVING
15 mins	6 hrs	4

INGREDIENTS	DIRECTIONS
<ul><li>two cups flaxseeds</li><li>two cups water</li><li>quarter cup low sodium soy sauce</li><li>2 tbsp. Sesame seeds</li><li>Sea salt and black pepper, as required</li><li>one and a half tbsps. Fresh lime juice</li></ul>	1. Cover flax seeds with water and soak for 1-2 hrs. Mixture should be gooey, but not too thin. Add more water to achieve this texture. 2. Mix in the remainder of the components. 3. Spread the solution about 1/8-inch-thick on dehydrator sheets. 4. Set the temperature to 105-115 degrees F and dehydrate 4-6 hrs. Flip over mixture and dehydrate another 4-6 hrs. Break crackers into large pieces after dehydrating.

PER SERVING			
Calories: 133kcal	Fat: 8.2g	Carbs: 7.1g	Protein: 4.6g

HAZELNUT LEMON CRACKERS

PREPARATION TIME	COOKING TIME	SERVING
15 mins	7 hrs	4

INGREDIENTS	DIRECTIONS
<ul><li>½ cup chia seeds</li><li>one cup water</li><li>3 cups hazelnuts, soaked overnight, skins removed</li><li>1 ½ tbsp. Lemon zest</li><li>1 tbsp. Maple syrup</li></ul>	1. Mix chia seeds in 1 cup water then let soften. 2. Remove soaked hazelnuts then drain them. Place hazelnuts in food processor then grind until fine.

- ½ tsp. Sea salt
- Black pepper, as required

3. Pour ground nuts into a container then combine with chia seeds, lemon zest, maple syrup, salt and pepper.
4. Spread onto dehydrator trays. Use a spatula to flatten dough to approximately ¼ inch thick. Dehydrate at 145 degrees F for 1 hour. Decrease heat to 115 and continue to dehydrate for 8 hrs.

PER SERVING

Calories: 169kcal	Fat: 15.6g	Carbs: 5.5g	Protein: 4.4g

MINT-SCENTED CHOCOLATE CHIP COOKIES

PREPARATION TIME	COOKING TIME	SERVING
15 mins	6 hrs	4

INGREDIENTS	DIRECTIONS
<ul><li>1 ½ cups almond meal</li><li>1 ½ cups ground pecans</li><li>1 cup cocoa powder</li><li>half cup cacao nibs</li><li>½ cup maple syrup</li><li>3 tbsp. Coconut oil</li><li>one tsp. Peppermint extract</li><li>one teaspoon Vanilla extract</li><li>one tbsp. Almond milk</li><li>½ teaspoon Salt</li></ul>	1. Place the entire components inside mixing bowl then pulse till mixed. Ingredients should form a cohesive dough. 2. Roll out dough to about ¼ inch thickness. 3. Cut out circles using a small glass. Alternatively, skip this process, roll dough into balls and flatten into disks. 4. Dehydrate for 24 hrs at 115 degrees F.

PER SERVING

Calories: 140kcal	Fat: 12.1g	Carbs: 8.8g	Protein: 4.3g

MACADAMIA-SAGE CRACKERS

PREPARATION TIME	COOKING TIME	SERVING
15 mins	6 hrs	4

INGREDIENTS	DIRECTIONS
• two cups macadamia nuts • two cups chia or flax seeds • 1 ½ tbsp. Fresh sage, crushed • Sea salt and white pepper, as required • three cups water • ½ cup olive oil	1. Put macadamia nuts and flax seeds into a food processor then grind into a flour. Add sage, salt and pepper. Process until you have a fine texture. 2. In a huge container, add water to nut and seed mix then stir until thick. Don't pour all the water at once. Add little amounts until a soft dough forms. 3. Spread onto dehydrator sheets. Drizzle with olive oil then drizzle additional sea salt. 4. Dehydrate at 110 deg. F for 4 hrs. Score the crackers, flip them over then dehydrate another 8 hrs.

PER SERVING

Calories: 176kcal	Fat: 15.1g	Carbs: 7.2g	Protein: 4.2g

FRUIT N' NUT BALLS

PREPARATION TIME	COOKING TIME	SERVING
15 mins	6 hrs	4

INGREDIENTS	DIRECTIONS
• half cup dried dates • ½ cup figs • ½ cup dried cherries • ½ cup dried apricots • ½ cup dried cranberries • 1 cup crushed pecans • 1 cup crushed almonds • 3 tsp. Coconut oil, melted • 1 cup flaked coconut	1. Finely process dates, figs, cherries, apricots and cranberries in a food processor. Mix with nuts and coconut oil in a container. 2. Shape into 1" balls and roll balls in coconut. 3. Place in dehydrator at 135 degrees F for 6 hrs.

PER SERVING

Calories: 102kcal	Fat: 8.4g	Carbs: 6.9g	Protein: 2g

SESAME SEED CRISPS

PREPARATION TIME	COOKING TIME	SERVING
15 mins	6 hrs	4

INGREDIENTS	DIRECTIONS
• half cup flax seeds • one cup water • half cup sesame seeds, toasted • ½ cup black sesame seeds • ½ tsp. Sea salt • ½ tsp. Dried thyme • ½ tsp. Garlic powder	1. In a container, mix seeds and seasonings with water. Stir till the mixture is well incorporated then leave for 10-15 mins to allow seeds to become pudding-like. 2. Spread onto dehydrator trays. Batter should be less than ¼ inch thick. Dehydrate at 110 degrees F for 8-12 hrs. Flip them over and dehydrate for another 8 hrs.

PER SERVING

Calories: 147kcal	Fat: 11.4g	Carbs: 6.8g	Protein: 4.8g

GRAHAM CRACKERS

PREPARATION TIME	COOKING TIME	SERVING
15 mins	6 hrs	4

INGREDIENTS	DIRECTIONS
• 4 cups almond flour • one cup oat flour • ½ cup flax seeds • ½ cup almond milk • one cup maple syrup • one tablespoon Vanilla • one tablespoon Cinnamon	1. Mix all the ingredients into the food processor. 2. Spread onto dehydrator trays. Make sure graham cracker mixture is about 1/8" thick. Dehydrate at 115 deg. F for 4 hrs. 3. Cut into squares then flip and dehydrate for 6 more hrs.

PER SERVING

Calories: 142kcal	Fat: 10.2g	Carbs: 9.6g	Protein: 5g

SWEET COCOA CHIA BARS

PREPARATION TIME	COOKING TIME	SERVING
15 mins	6 hrs	4

INGREDIENTS	DIRECTIONS
<ul><li>one cup chia seeds</li><li>two cups water</li><li>¼ cup cocoa powder</li><li>6 figs, chopped</li><li>1 apple, peeled, cored and chopped</li><li>1 cup walnuts, chopped</li><li>3 tbsp. Honey</li><li>3 tbsp. Cacao nibs</li></ul>	1. Soak chia seeds in ½ cup of water for 30 mins. Drain. 2. Blend all remaining ingredients in a blender, except for cacao nibs. Add little amount of water to achieve the right consistency. 3. Stir together chia seeds, blended mixture and cacao nibs. 4. Allow to rest for 20-25 mins. 5. Spread the mixture onto dehydrator tray. Dehydrate for 1 hour at 135 degrees F. Cut into bars. 6. Lower temperature to 110 degrees and dehydrate another 8 hrs. Flip bars and dehydrate another 8 hrs.

PER SERVING

Calories: 125kcal	Fat: 9.6g	Carbs: 5.6g	Protein: 5.2g

CHAPTER 8: Recipes for Complete Lunch

GROUND BEEF AND BEANS CHILI

PREPARATION TIME	COOKING TIME	SERVING
10 mins	10 hrs	3

INGREDIENTS	DIRECTIONS
<ul><li>1 big white onion, peeled, sliced</li><li>one pound ground beef</li><li>15 ounces cooked red beans</li><li>½ cup ground bread crumbs</li><li>½ teaspoon minced garlic</li><li>14 ounces diced tomatoes</li><li>¾ teaspoon salt</li><li>3 tablespoons red chili powder</li><li>10 ounces tomato puree</li></ul>	1. Use a big container, put ground beef in it, include bread crumbs and afterwards mix till blended, put away till essential. 2. Use a medium pot, put it across moderate flame, include oil & once warm, include onion and garlic, and cook for five mins till softened. 3. Include ground beef, cook it for 10 mins or till browned, afterwards stir in red chili powder and cook for 1 minute. 4. Add beans, tomatoes, and tomato puree, stir till combined and boil the chili for one hr till cooked. 5. When done, eliminate the pan from flame and allow the chili cool for ten mins. 6. Then turn on the dehydrator, afterwards set it to 145 deg. F, and allow it to warm up. 7. In the meantime, line the dehydrator trays with parchment paper and then disperse chili in a thin layer on each tray. 8. Place the dehydrator trays in the preheated dehydrator, shut with its lid, and then let the chili dry for 8 to 10 hrs until completely dry and crumbly. 9. When done, turn off the dehydrator, open the lid and let the chili cool for 30 mins at room temperature. 10. Break chili into small pieces, transfer evenly between three plastic bags, and store in a cool and dry place, away from heat or direct light. 11. When ready to eat, place a medium pot over medium heat, add a bag of chili in it, pour in

11. 1 cup water, stir in oil and then raise it towards a boil.

12. Then turn heat to moderate level, cook the chili for 1 minute or till rehydrate, and serve with pita chips.

PER SERVING

Calories: 342.3kcal	Fat: 19.1g	Carbs: 25.5g	Protein: 18.1g

TACO STEW

PREPARATION TIME	COOKING TIME	SERVING
10 mins	12 hrs	4

INGREDIENTS	DIRECTIONS
<ul><li>14 ounces cooked black beans</li><li>2.2 pounds ground turkey</li><li>1 medium red onion, peeled, chopped</li><li>12 ounces sweet corn</li><li>2 medium red bell pepper, cored, chopped</li><li>14 ounces diced tomatoes</li><li>1 bunch of cilantro, destemmed, leaves chopped</li><li>one tsp. salt</li><li>two tsps. taco spice mixture</li><li>one tbsp. olive oil</li><li>one tbsp. powdered dehydrated cheddar cheese</li><li>Corn chips, crumbled, for serving</li></ul>	1. Grab a big pot and put it across moderate flame. Once the oil is warm, include the onion and continue to simmer for another five minutes, or till the onion has become more tender. 2. Include ground turkey, whisk till combined, cook for 10 mins until browned and then transfer meat mixture to a colander for draining it well. 3. Then return turkey mixture into the saucepan, add beans, corn, and red pepper, stir in taco spice mix and continue cooking for 5 mins. 4. Add tomatoes along with their juice, mix till combined, raise the mixture to a simmer and afterwards stir in cilantro. 5. Season the mixture with salt, turn flame to the low level, and then cook for fifteen mins, concealing the pot using a cover. 6. After 15 mins, eliminate the pot from flame and then allow it to cool entirely. 7. Then turn on the dehydrator, afterwards set it to 145 deg. F, and allow it to warm up. 8. In the meantime, line the dehydrator trays with parchment paper and then disperse stew in a fine layer on each tray.

9. Place the dehydrator trays in the preheated dehydrator, shut with its lid, and then let the chili dry for 8 to 12 hrs until completely dry and brittle.

10. When done, turn off the dehydrator, open the cover and let the stew cool for 30 mins at room temperature.

11. Transfer the stew evenly among four plastic bags, pack cheese in separate plastic bags and then store in a cool and dry place, away from heat or direct light.

12. When ready to eat, place stew from one plastic bag in a medium pot, pour in 1 cup water, put the pot across moderate flame and then raise it towards a boil.

13. Bring the stew to a boil, cook it for 5 mins, remove the pot from heat and then let the stew stand for 5 mins or until rehydrated.

14. Stir in the cheese, garnish with corn chips and then serve.

PER SERVING

Calories: 532kcal	Fat: 19.4g	Carbs: 31g	Protein: 58.6g

RED LENTIL CHILI

PREPARATION TIME	COOKING TIME	SERVING
5 mins	10 hrs and 30 mins	4

INGREDIENTS	DIRECTIONS
<ul><li>one cup red lentils, uncooked</li><li>14 ounces cooked kidney beans</li><li>2 cups sliced zucchini</li><li>14 ounces diced tomatoes, fire-roasted</li><li>1 cup diced green bell pepper</li><li>1 cup diced white onion</li><li>3 tsps. crushed garlic</li><li>one tsp. salt</li><li>3 tablespoons red chili powder</li><li>one tbsp. ground cumin</li></ul>	1. Grab a big saucepan and put it across moderate flame. Once the oil is warm, include the onion and bell pepper. Top using one tsp. of salt, and afterwards continue to simmer for seven to ten mins till the vegetables have become softer. 2. Include zucchini, cook for 10 mins or until vegetables are softened, stir in garlic, red chili powder and cumin and then continue cooking for 30 seconds until fragrant.

- one tsp. sugar
- two tbsps. tomato paste
- one tbsp. olive oil
- 2 cups vegetable broth

3. Add beans and tomatoes, stir in tomato paste, put in the broth, mix till combined, and then raise it to a simmer.
4. Add lentils, simmer the chili for 20 mins until lentils have turned tender, and then stir in sugar; taste to adjust the seasoning.
5. Eliminate the pot from the flame and allow it to cool for 10 mins.
6. Meanwhile, turn on the dehydrator, afterwards set it to 135 deg. F, and allow it to warm up.
7. In the meantime, line the dehydrator trays with parchment paper and then disperses chili inside a thin layer on each tray.
8. Place the dehydrator trays in the preheated dehydrator, shut with its lid, and then let the chili dry for 8 to 12 hrs until completely dry and crumbly.
9. When done, turn off the dehydrator, open the lid and let the chili cool for 30 mins at room temperature.
10. Break chili into small pieces, transfer evenly between four plastic bags, and store in a cool and dry place, away from heat or direct light.
11. When ready to eat, place a medium pot over medium heat, add a bag of chili in it, pour in 1 cup water, stir in oil and then bring it to a boil.
12. Then turn flame to moderate level, cook the chili for 10 mins till lentils and beans have turned softer and serve.

PER SERVING

| Calories: 797kcal | Fat: 24g | Carbs: 122g | Protein: 36g |

VEGETABLE YELLOW CURRY

PREPARATION TIME	COOKING TIME	SERVING
5 mins	8 hrs and 10 mins	2

INGREDIENTS

- 1 ½ cup cooked white rice, cooled
- 2 cups frozen vegetable mix
- 1 tablespoon Thai yellow curry paste
- 4 tablespoons coconut milk powder

DIRECTIONS

1. Switch on the dehydrator, then set it to 135 degrees F, and let it preheat.
2. Meanwhile, line the dehydrator trays with parchment paper and then spread rice, vegetables, and curry paste in a thin layer separately on each tray.
3. Place the dehydrator trays in the preheated dehydrator, shut with its lid, and then let the chili dry for 4 to 8 hrs until completely dry.
4. When done, turn off the dehydrator, open the lid and let the rice, vegetables, and curry paste cool for 30 mins at room temperature.
5. Divide rice, vegetables, and curry paste evenly among four plastic bags, add coconut milk powder, and store in a cool and dry place, away from heat or direct light.
6. When ready to eat, one packet of rice, vegetables and curry paste in a moderate pot, put it across moderate-high flame, put in 2 cups water, and afterwards bring the mixture to a boil.
7. Then switch heat to medium-low heat, cook for 5 mins, remove the pot from heat and let the mixture for 5 to 10 mins until rehydrated.

PER SERVING

Calories: 445kcal	Fat: 17.2g	Carbs: 61.1g	Protein: 7.6g

BEEF AND BEAN CHILI

PREPARATION TIME	COOKING TIME	SERVING
15 mins	10 hrs	5

INGREDIENTS	DIRECTIONS
<ul><li>one and a quarter pound ground beef, lean</li><li>½ cup breadcrumbs, finely ground</li><li>1 onion, large</li><li>2 cloves garlic</li><li>3 tablespoons chili powder</li><li>1 can kidney beans, drained</li><li>1 can tomato puree</li><li>1 can diced tomatoes</li></ul>	1. Combine ground beef and breadcrumbs. Set aside. 2. Sauté onion and garlic in a pan coated with olive oil. 3. Add ground beef mixed with breadcrumbs. Cook for 10 mins. Add chili powder. Cook for a min. Include drained beans, tomato puree and diced tomatoes. Cook until bubbling. 4. Simmer for 1 hour. 5. Spread chili on dehydrator tray lined with parchment paper. Dry for 10 hrs at 125 deg. F. 6. Divide into 1 cup servings and pack in resealable bags. 7. To Rehydrate: Combine 1 cup chili with 1 cup water. Let sit for 5 mins. Bring to a boil. Cook for 1 minute.

PER SERVING			
Calories: 382kcal	Fat: 11g	Carbs: 39g	Protein: 33g

ROOT BARK STEW

PREPARATION TIME	COOKING TIME	SERVING
15 mins	20 hrs	4

INGREDIENTS	DIRECTIONS
<ul><li>1 large sweet potato</li><li>1-pound parsnips</li><li>1 large rutabaga</li><li>3 medium turnips</li><li>two average onions, sliced</li><li>two cloves garlic, crushed</li></ul>	1. To make root bark stew with chicken recipe, just add ¼ cup dried chicken when rehydrating. Dry root bark can also be eaten as is, as a snack. 2. Peel and dice roots into ½-inch cubes. 3. Sauté onion for 5 mins in non-stick pan over medium-high heat.

- 16 ounces chicken broth
- 1 can diced tomatoes, drained
- ¼ cup raisins
- 1 tablespoon curry powder
- 1 tablespoon ground cumin
- 1 tablespoon olive oil
- 1 teaspoon cinnamon
- Salt and pepper to taste

4. Add garlic, curry, cumin, cinnamon and a splash of chicken broth. Stir for another minute.
5. In a large pot, put the contents of the pan. Add diced roots and raisins.
6. Add enough chicken broth to cover roots.
7. Bring to a boil. Reduce heat. Cover and simmer for 10 mins. Stir occasionally.
8. Add diced tomatoes, salt and pepper. Simmer for 5 more mins.
9. Drain off broth into pot.
10. To make the bark - Put broth and 4 cups of cooked roots into a blender. Blend until smooth.
11. Spread ¼-inch thick mixture on the dehydrator tray lined with drying sheet.
12. Dry for 8 hrs at 135 deg. F.
13. Put remaining cooked roots on the dehydrator tray.
14. Dry for 12 hrs at 135 deg. F.
15. Let cool before packing. Combine roots and bark into individual meal servings and pack in plastic bags.
16. To Rehydrate: Combine ¾ cup dried root pieces, ¼ cup dried root bark and 1 cup water. Soak for 5 mins. Bring to a boil. Cook for 1 minute.

PER SERVING			
Calories: 301kcal	Fat: 5g	Carbs: 62g	Protein: 7g

RATATOUILLE

PREPARATION TIME	COOKING TIME	SERVING
15 mins	10 hrs	5

INGREDIENTS	DIRECTIONS
<ul><li>two onions, diced</li><li>one small zucchinis, diced</li><li>1 eggplant, diced</li></ul>	1. To enjoy ratatouille with rice or macaroni, combine ½ cup ratatouille, ½ cup dried rice or macaroni and 1 cup water. Bring to a boil for 1 minute. Let sit for 10 mins.

- 1 red pepper, diced
- 1 yellow pepper, diced
- 2 cups fresh tomatoes
- 2 garlic cloves, smashed
- 2 bay leaves
- 4 teaspoons olive oil
- one tsp. dried thyme
- one tsp. fennel seeds

2. Peel the eggplant. Slice diagonally into ½-inch slices. Squeeze to remove excess liquid.
3. Dice eggplant and the rest of the vegetables into small pieces.
4. Sauté onion for 5 in a non-stick pan.
5. Add garlic, peppers, fennel, bay leaves and thyme. Sauté until peppers are soft.
6. Add eggplant. Sauté until it turns golden.
7. Add zucchini. Sauté for another 5 mins.
8. Add diced tomatoes, salt and pepper. Reduce the heat. Simmer for 15 mins.
9. Spread vegetables on the dehydrator tray lined with drying sheet.
10. Dry for 10 hrs at 135 deg. F.
11. Let cool before packing. Divide into individual servings and pack in plastic bags.
12. To Rehydrate: Combine 1 cup ratatouille with 1 cup water. Rehydrate for 10 mins. Heat until warm.

PER SERVING			
Calories: 118kcal	**Fat:** 4g	**Carbs:** 19g	**Protein:** 3g

CURRY RICE WITH CHICKEN AND CASHEWS

PREPARATION TIME	COOKING TIME	SERVING
10 mins	23 hrs	2

INGREDIENTS	DIRECTIONS
<ul><li>2/3 cup instant brown rice</li><li>half cup chicken, chopped, dried and frozen</li><li>¼ cup cashews, roasted and chopped</li><li>¼ cup mixed vegetables, dried and frozen</li><li>1 ½ teaspoon chicken flavor base, powdered</li><li>1 ½ teaspoon curry powder</li><li>1 teaspoon chia seeds</li></ul>	1. Dehydrate each ingredient that needs to be dried separately: chicken and mixed vegetables. Follow required time and temperature for each. Chicken – dry for 12 hrs at 125 deg. F, Mixed vegetables – dry for 11 hrs at 125 deg. F 2. To Assemble: Add all ingredients except the water in a resealable bag. Store until ready to use. 3. To Rehydrate: Bring water to a boil. Rest the resealable bag on a container. Open and

- 1 teaspoon onion flakes, dried
- ¼ teaspoon garlic powder
- ¼ teaspoon salt
- 1/8 teaspoon black pepper, ground
- 1 ½ cup water

pour in boiling water. Seal. Soak for 9 mins. Turn upside down to mix.

4. Transfer to a container.

PER SERVING

Calories: 427kcal	Fat: 12g	Carbs: 66g	Protein: 15g

THAI PEANUT NOODLES WITH CHICKEN AND VEGETABLES

PREPARATION TIME	COOKING TIME	SERVING
10 mins	23 hrs	4

INGREDIENTS	DIRECTIONS
<ul><li>1 cup pasta</li><li>¼ cup chicken, chopped, dried and frozen</li><li>¼ cup peanuts, roasted and chopped</li><li>¼ cup mixed vegetables, dried and frozen</li><li>2 tablespoons peanut butter, powdered</li><li>1 ½ teaspoon chicken flavor base, powdered</li><li>1 ½ teaspoon cilantro, dried and frozen</li><li>1 teaspoon chia seeds</li><li>¼ teaspoon garlic powder</li><li>¼ teaspoon ginger, ground</li><li>¼ teaspoon salt</li><li>1/8 teaspoon black pepper, ground</li><li>Pinch of cayenne pepper, ground</li><li>1 cup water</li></ul>	1. Dehydrate each ingredient that needs to be dried separately: chicken and mixed vegetables. Follow required time and temperature for each. Chicken – dry for 12 hrs at 125 deg. F, Mixed vegetables – dry for 11 hrs at 125 deg. F. 2. To Assemble: Add all ingredients except the water in a resealable bag. Store until ready to use. 3. To Rehydrate: Bring water to a boil. Rest the resealable bag on a container. Open and pour in boiling water. Seal. Soak for 9 mins. Turn upside down to mix. 4. Transfer to a container.

PER SERVING

Calories: 283kcal	Fat: 13g	Carbs: 31g	Protein: 13g

FIESTA RICE WITH CORN AND CHICKEN

PREPARATION TIME	COOKING TIME	SERVING
10 mins	32 hrs	2

INGREDIENTS

- 2/3 cup instant brown rice
- one-third cup chicken, chopped, dried and frozen
- ½ cup corn, dried and frozen
- ¼ cup tomatoes, chopped, dried and frozen
- 1 ½ teaspoon chicken flavor base, powdered
- one and a half tsp. chili powder
- one tsp. chia seeds
- one tsp. onion flakes, dried
- half tsp. cilantro, dried and frozen
- ¼ teaspoon cumin
- ¼ tsp. garlic powder
- ¼ tsp. jalapeno, minced and dried
- ¼ teaspoon oregano, dried
- ¼ tsp. salt
- 1/8 tsp. black pepper, ground
- 1 ½ cup water

DIRECTIONS

1. Dehydrate each ingredient that needs to be dried separately: chicken, corn and tomatoes. Follow required time and temperature for each. Chicken – dry for 12 hrs at 125 deg. F, Corn – dry for 12 hrs at 135 deg. F, Tomatoes – dry for 8 hrs at 135 deg. F.
2. To Assemble: Add all ingredients except the water in a resealable bag. Store until ready to use.
3. To Rehydrate: Bring water to a boil. Rest the resealable bag on a container. Open and pour in boiling water. Seal. Soak for 9 mins. Turn upside down to mix.
4. Transfer to a container.

PER SERVING

Calories: 383kcal	Fat: 6g	Carbs: 69g	Protein: 14g

CREAMY ALFREDO NOODLES WITH CHICKEN, MUSHROOMS AND PINE NUTS

PREPARATION TIME	COOKING TIME	SERVING
10 mins	26 hrs	4

INGREDIENTS	DIRECTIONS
<ul><li>1 cup pasta</li><li>¼ cup chicken, chopped, dried and frozen</li><li>¼ cup pine nuts, toasted</li><li>¼ cup mushrooms, chopped, dried and frozen</li><li>3 tablespoons Parmesan cheese, grated</li><li>2 tablespoons instant dried buttermilk powder</li><li>2 tablespoons cornstarch</li><li>1 ½ teaspoon chicken flavor base, powdered</li><li>1 teaspoon chia seeds</li><li>¾ teaspoon dried Italian herb blend</li><li>¼ teaspoon garlic powder</li><li>¼ teaspoon salt</li><li>1/8 teaspoon black pepper, ground</li><li>1 ¼ cup water</li></ul>	1. Dehydrate each ingredient that needs to be dried separately: chicken and mushrooms. Follow required time and temperature for each. Chicken – dry for 12 hrs at 125 deg. F, Mushrooms – dry for 14 hrs at 130 deg. F. 2. To Assemble: Add all ingredients except the water in a resealable bag. Store until ready to use. 3. To Rehydrate: Bring water to a boil. Rest the resealable bag on a container. Open and pour in boiling water. Seal. Soak for 9 mins. Turn upside down to mix. 4. Transfer to a container.

PER SERVING			
Calories: 227kcal	**Fat:** 8g	**Carbs:** 28g	**Protein:** 11g

COUSCOUS WITH CHICKEN AND VEGETABLES

PREPARATION TIME	COOKING TIME	SERVING
10 mins	23 hrs	2

INGREDIENTS

- one-third cup whole wheat couscous
- one-third cup chicken, chopped, dried and frozen
- ½ cup mixed vegetables, dried and frozen
- 1 ½ teaspoon chicken flavor base, powdered
- 1 teaspoon chia seeds
- 1 teaspoon onion flakes, dried
- ¼ teaspoon dried parsley
- ¼ teaspoon dried thyme
- ¼ teaspoon garlic powder
- ¼ teaspoon sage
- ¼ teaspoon salt
- 1/8 teaspoon black pepper, ground
- 1 ½ cup water

DIRECTIONS

1. Dehydrate each ingredient that needs to be dried separately: chicken and mixed vegetables. Follow required time and temperature for each. Chicken – dry for 12 hrs at 125 deg. F, Mixed vegetables – dry for 11 hrs at 125 deg. F.
2. To Assemble: Add all ingredients except the water in a resealable bag. Store until ready to use.
3. To Rehydrate: Bring water to a boil. Rest the resealable bag on a container. Open and pour in boiling water. Seal. Soak for 9 mins. Turn upside down to mix.
4. Transfer to a container.

PER SERVING

Calories: 156kcal	Fat: 2g	Carbs: 25g	Protein: 10g

30-Day Meal Plan

Days	Breakfast	Lunch	Dinner	Snacks
1	Raw Zucchini Bread	Chicken Jerky	Spinach Balls	Sweet Kale Chips
2	Vegan Bread	Vegetable Yellow Curry	Cajun Fish Jerky	Vegan Broccoli Crisps
3	Black Bread	Trout Jerky	Ranch Brussels Sprout Skins	Garlic Zucchini Chips
4	Apple and Nut "Raw" Cereal	Ratatouille	Paprika Pork Jerky	Zucchini Snacks
5	Almond Cranberry Cookies	Fish Teriyaki Jerky	Lemon Salmon Jerky	Pear Chips
6	Mint-Scented Chocolate Chip Cookies	Flavorful Turkey Jerky	Spiced Cucumbers	Crunch Green Bean Chips
7	Fruit N' Nut Balls	Mustard Beef Jerky with Balsamic Vinegar	Maple Carrot Straws	Cucumber Chips
8	Sweet Cocoa Chia Bars	Fiesta Rice with Corn and Chicken	Flavorful Teriyaki Jerky	Cinnamon Apple Chips
9	Sesame Seed Crisps	Couscous with Chicken and Vegetables	Soy Marinated Salmon Jerky	Beet Chips
10	Banana Breakfast Crepes	Pork Jerky in Chipotle Sauce	Dehydrated Corn	Pumpkin Chips
11	Apple Cinnamon Graham Cookies	Lemon Pepper Fish Jerky	Root Vegetable Medley	Sweet Potato Chips
12	Orange-Scented Granola with Dried Blueberries	Shrimp	Sweet & Smoky Salmon Jerky	Banana Chips
13	Graham Crackers	Ground Beef and Beans Chili	Beer Beef Jerky	Eggplant Chips
14	Flax Seed Crackers	Beef and Bean Chili	Ranch Brussels Sprout Skins	Green Apple Chips
15	Macadamia-Sage Crackers	Barbecue Beef Jerky	Paprika Pork Jerky	Pickle Chips
16	Hazelnut Lemon Crackers	Venison Jerky	Lemon Salmon Jerky	Potato Chips
17	Seaweed & Tamari Crackers	Beef Jerky	Spiced Cucumbers	Banana Cocoa Leather
18	Sesame & Carrot Crackers	Thai Peanut Noodles with Chicken and Vegetables	Perfect Lamb Jerky	Goji Berry Leather
19	Peanut Butter & Banana Crackers	Curry Rice with Chicken and Cashews	Tuna	Tasty Pineapple Chunks
20	Green Crackers	Sweet & Spicy Beef Jerky	Maple Carrot Straws	Peach Cobbler
21	Mexican Crackers	Taco Stew	Flavorful Teriyaki Jerky	Carrot Cake
22	Nothing But Fruit Bars	Creamy Alfredo Noodles with Chicken, Mushrooms and Pine Nuts	Hickory Smoked Jerky	Dehydrated Beets
23	Banana Bread Pudding	Root Bark Stew	Beer Beef Jerky	Tex-Mex Green Beans
24	Mango Lime Fruit Leather	Easy Mexican Jerky	Ranch Brussels Sprout Skins	Moroccan Carrot Crunch
25	Apple Fig Fruit Leather	Red Lentil Chili	Asian Pork Jerky	Dehydrated Asparagus
26	Asian Pear and Ginger Treats	Ground Beef and Beans Chili	Buffalo Jerky	Dehydrated Tomatoes
27	Peach & Raspberry	Vegetable Yellow Curry	Paprika Pork Jerky	Dehydrated Okra
28	Fruit Drizzles	Beef Bulgogi Jerky	Lemon Salmon Jerky	Dried Cauliflower Popcorn
29	Strawberry Passion Fruit Leather	Turkey Jerky	Spiced Cucumbers	Dried Sweet Potato
30	Plum Fruit Leather	Root Bark Stew	Ranch Beef Jerky	Sweet and Savory Beet Rounds

Index

Conversion Chart

Volume Equivalents (Liquid)

US Standard	US Standard (ounces)	Metric (approximate)
2 tablespoons	1 fl. oz.	30 mL
¼ cup	2 fl. oz.	60 mL
½ cup	4 fl. oz.	120 mL
1 cup	8 fl. oz.	240 mL
1½ cups	12 fl. oz.	355 mL
2 cups or 1 pint	16 fl. oz.	475 mL
4 cups or 1 quart	32 fl. oz.	1 L
1 gallon	128 fl. oz.	4 L

Volume Equivalents (Dry)

US Standard	Metric (approximate)
⅛ teaspoon	0.5 mL
¼ teaspoon	1 mL
½ teaspoon	2 mL
¾ teaspoon	4 mL
1 teaspoon	5 mL
1 tablespoon	15 mL
¼ cup	59 mL
⅓ cup	79 mL
½ cup	118 mL
⅔ cup	156 mL
¾ cup	177 mL
1 cup	235 mL
2 cups or 1 pint	475 mL
3 cups	700 mL
4 cups or 1 quart	1 L

Oven Temperatures

Fahrenheit (F)	Celsius (C) (approximate)
250°F	120°C
300°F	150°C
325°F	165°C
350°F	180°C
375°F	190°C
400°F	200°C
425°F	220°C
450°F	230°C

Weight Equivalents

US Standard	Metric (approximate)
½ ounce	15g
1 ounce	30g
2 ounces	60g
4 ounces	115g
8 ounces	225g
12 ounces	340g
16 ounces or 1 pound	455g

Conclusion

Dehydrating is a great way to do a variety of things that will serve you in the long run. It is a great way to preserve surplus amounts of foods so that they remain in your possession for a longer period. Many people might have a misconception that storing food may make it less appetizing, but by concentrating the flavors, it increases the tastiness.

In the time of emergencies, you don't know what might come in handy. One thing you will need is a food supply. If you are going to a remote area where there are limited supplies and resources, dehydration can solve your problems. Hikers, campers, and even astronauts use this technique, so don't waste time and start dehydrating your food.

Most of us settle ourselves in our daily routine, not even thinking about doing something new due to fear. It's very healthy to engage in different activities, and there is no fear of dehydrating your food. It's perfectly safe, if not healthier, and can give you a range of flavors you have never tasted before.

I hope that you enjoy dehydrating and eating your food.

Good luck on your dehydrating journey!

Made in United States
Troutdale, OR
10/26/2024

24132149R10053